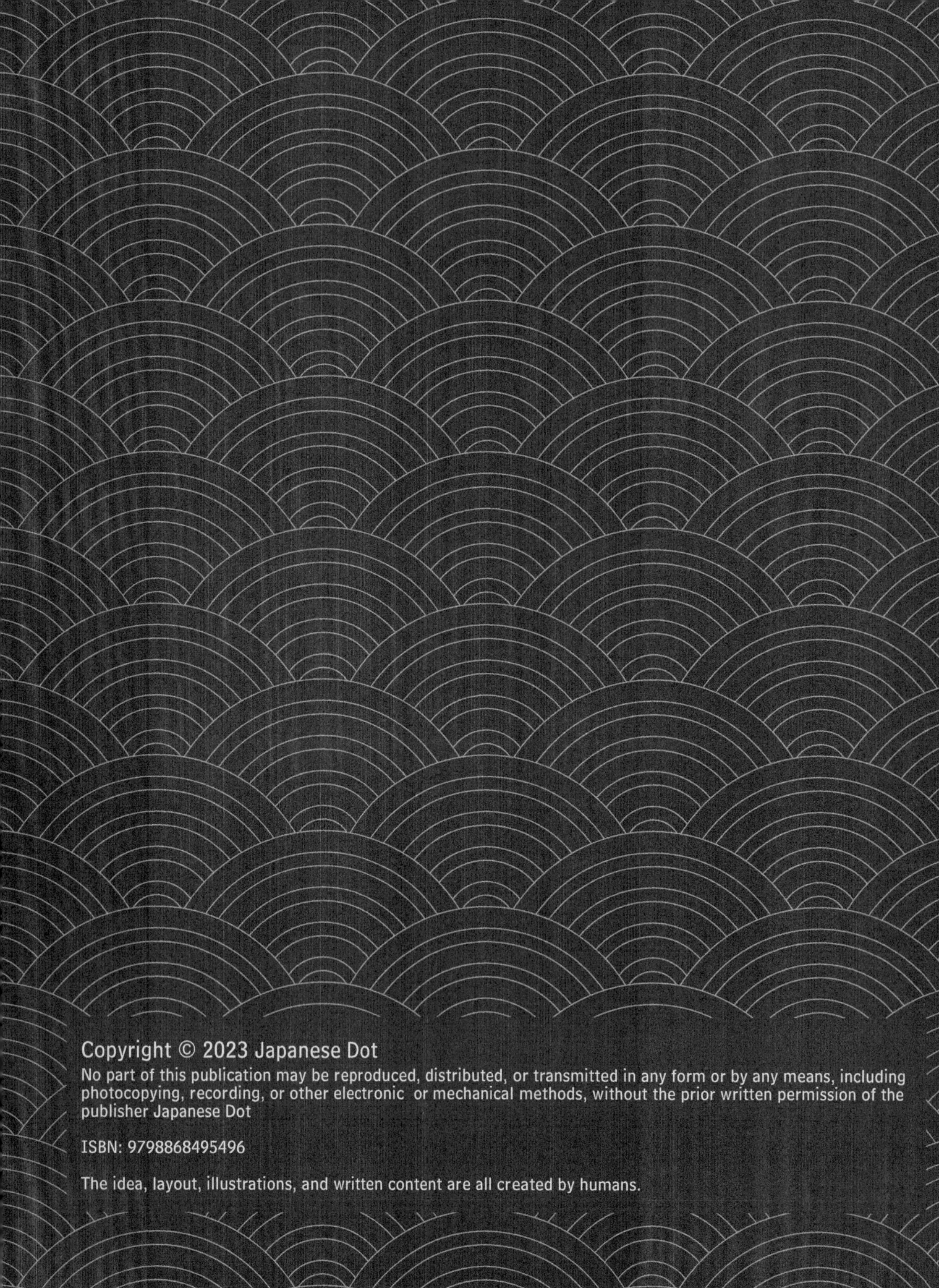

Copyright © 2023 Japanese Dot

No part of this publication may be reproduced, distributed, or transmitted in any form or by any means, including photocopying, recording, or other electronic or mechanical methods, without the prior written permission of the publisher Japanese Dot

ISBN: 9798868495496

The idea, layout, illustrations, and written content are all created by humans.

Japanese Pattern Glossary

Japanese kimono patterns are extremely beautiful. They reflect nature – plants, animals, landscapes. Their reference is to the seasons of the year. Patterns are often associated with special events, such as religious ceremonies and traditional holidays, family gatherings. Associated with each pattern is some kind of divination, good wishes, which is why they are called "auspicious patterns" – Kisshō mon'yō (吉祥文様). It is believed that applied to clothing, they bring good luck, blessings and success in business.

The following are some examples of such patterns:

The most well-known Japanese pattern is **Seigaiha (青海波)**, which translates to "blue ocean waves." It represents the tranquil nature of the sea and is often accompanied by other motifs.

such as **Chidori (千鳥)**, small birds flying over the calm sea,

and **Kumo (雲)** clouds.

When Seigaiha is combined with Chidori, it shows the peaceful coexistence of land and sea.

Sakura (桜): the second most famous pattern in Japanese decoration, featuring cherry blossoms and symbolizing Japan. The blooming Sakura represents the beginning of spring and the fleeting nature of life. The pink cherry blossoms symbolize the delicacy and transience of life.
Hannami, the cherry blossom festival, is celebrated in Japan in April.

Kiku (菊): featuring chrysanthemum flowers, has great significance in Japanese culture. It is closely associated with the Japanese imperial family and symbolizes power and high social status. Only the emperor and aristocracy were allowed to use this motif on their clothing and possessions. The chrysanthemum flower is also the national emblem of Japan.

Kikko (亀甲): this pattern is called **"tortoise pattern"** as it looks like a tortoise shell, and a tortoise is an animal that lives over 100 years and has a thick shell. Therefore, Kikko is a sign of longevity and protection from dangers

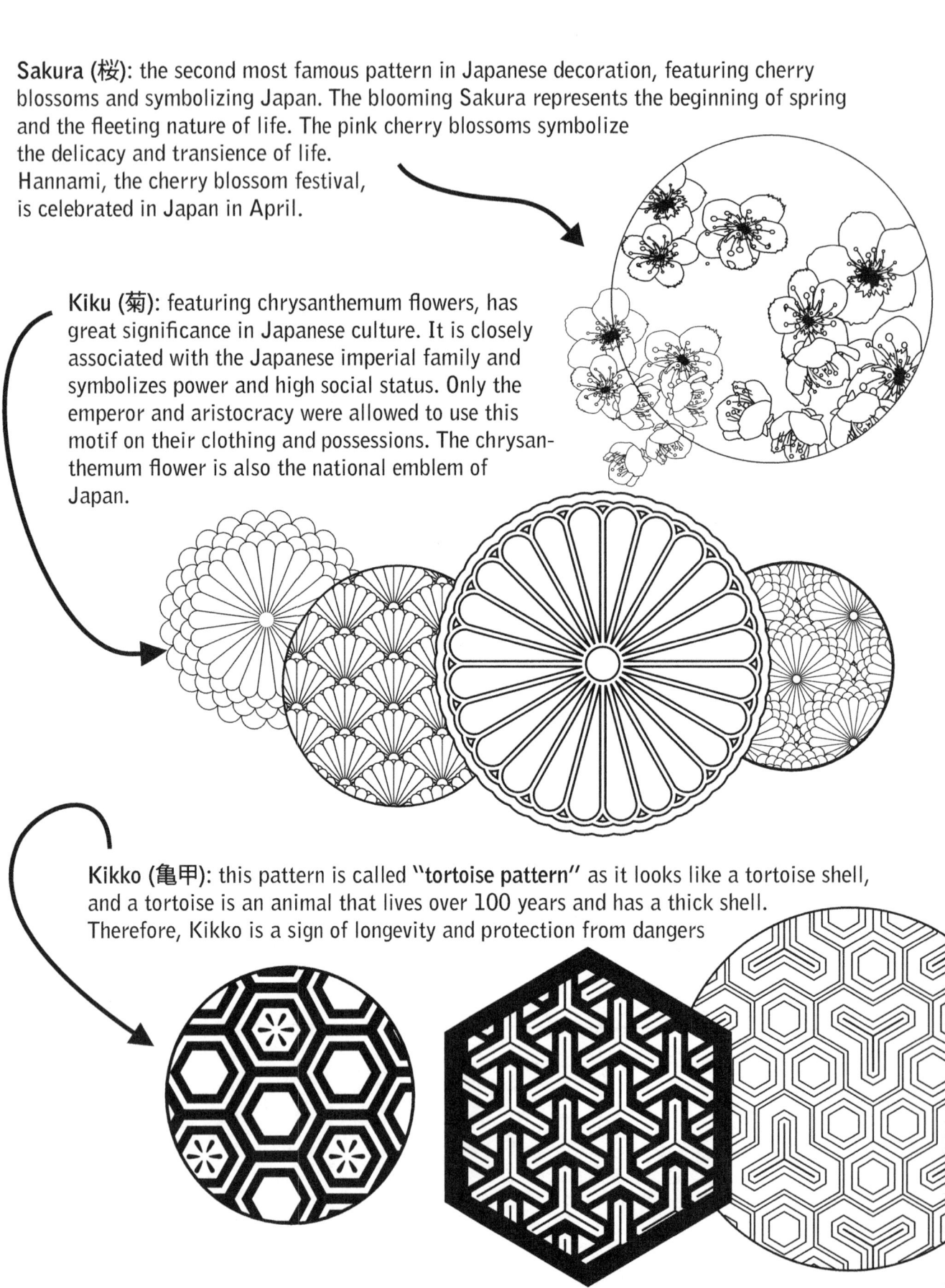

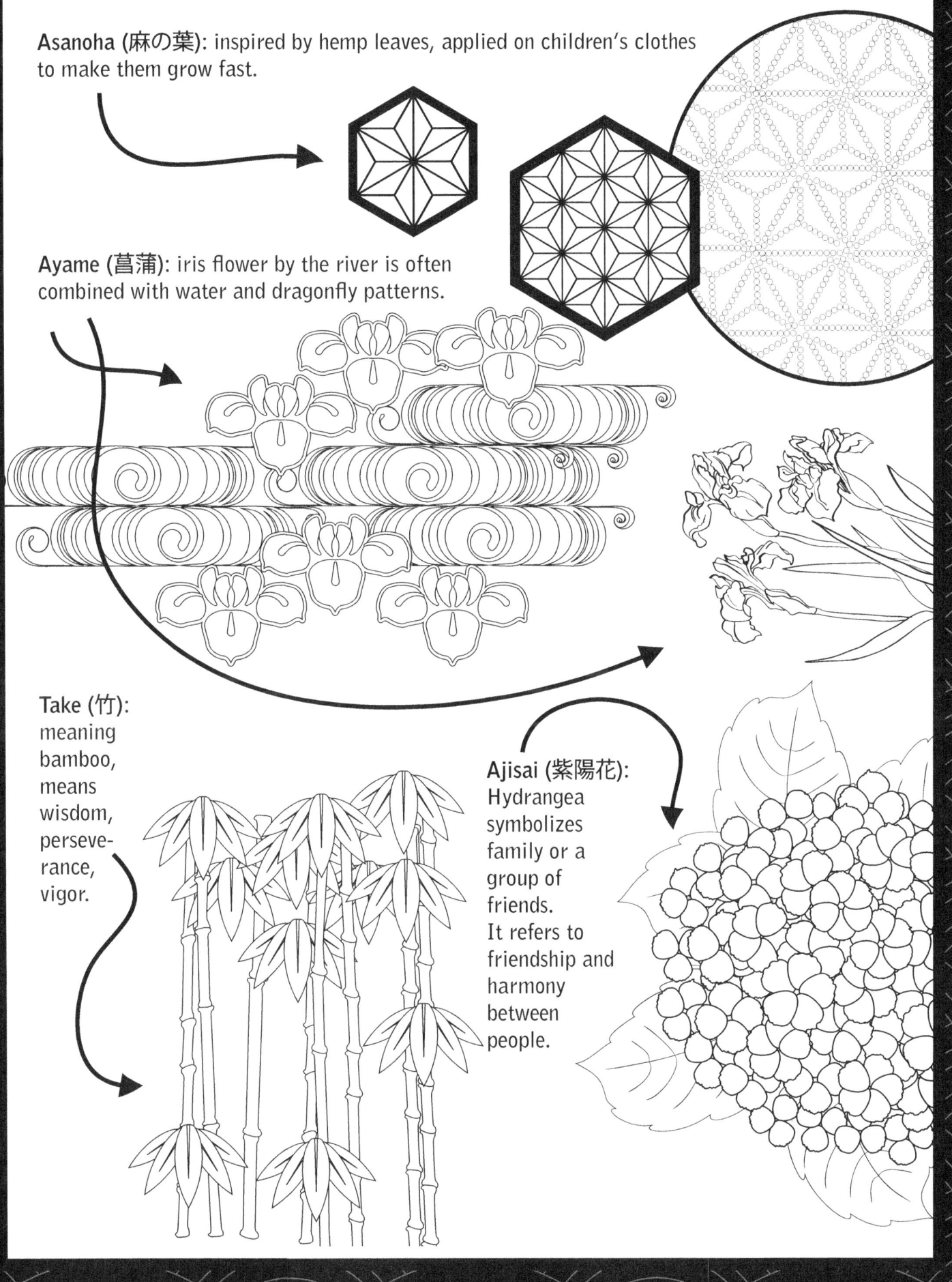

Momiji (紅葉): falling autumn maple leaves, expresses longing for a time gone by.

Matsu (松): the Japanese pine as it grows long and is a tree that does not resist rain, snow and frost. It symbolizes the hardiness and steadfastness of life.

Yukiwa (雪輪): snowflakes – a good clothing pattern for the snow holiday.

Tsuru (鶴): cranes, especially when in flight, symbolize happiness, a long and happy journey through life.

Ogi (扇): fan.

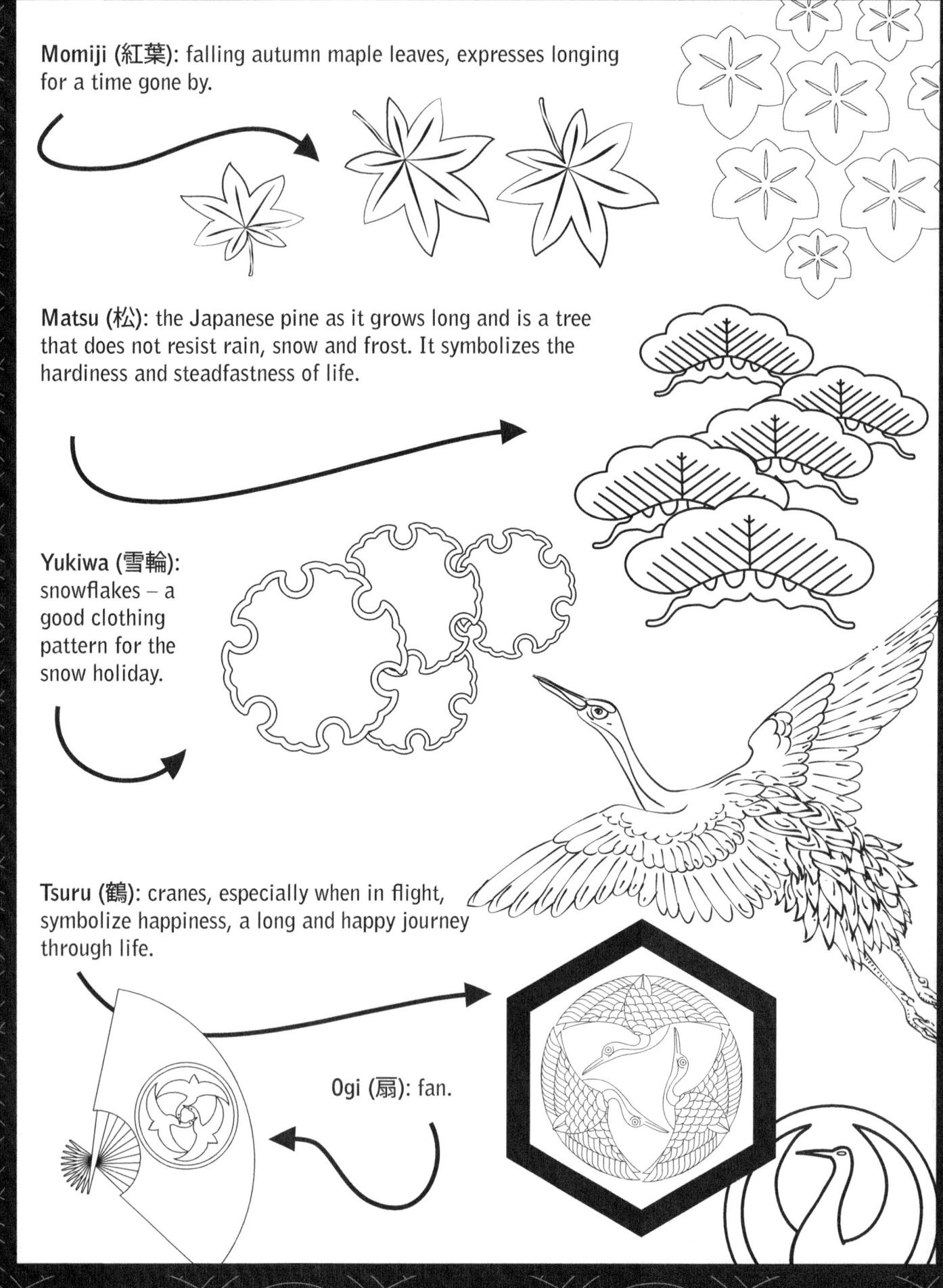

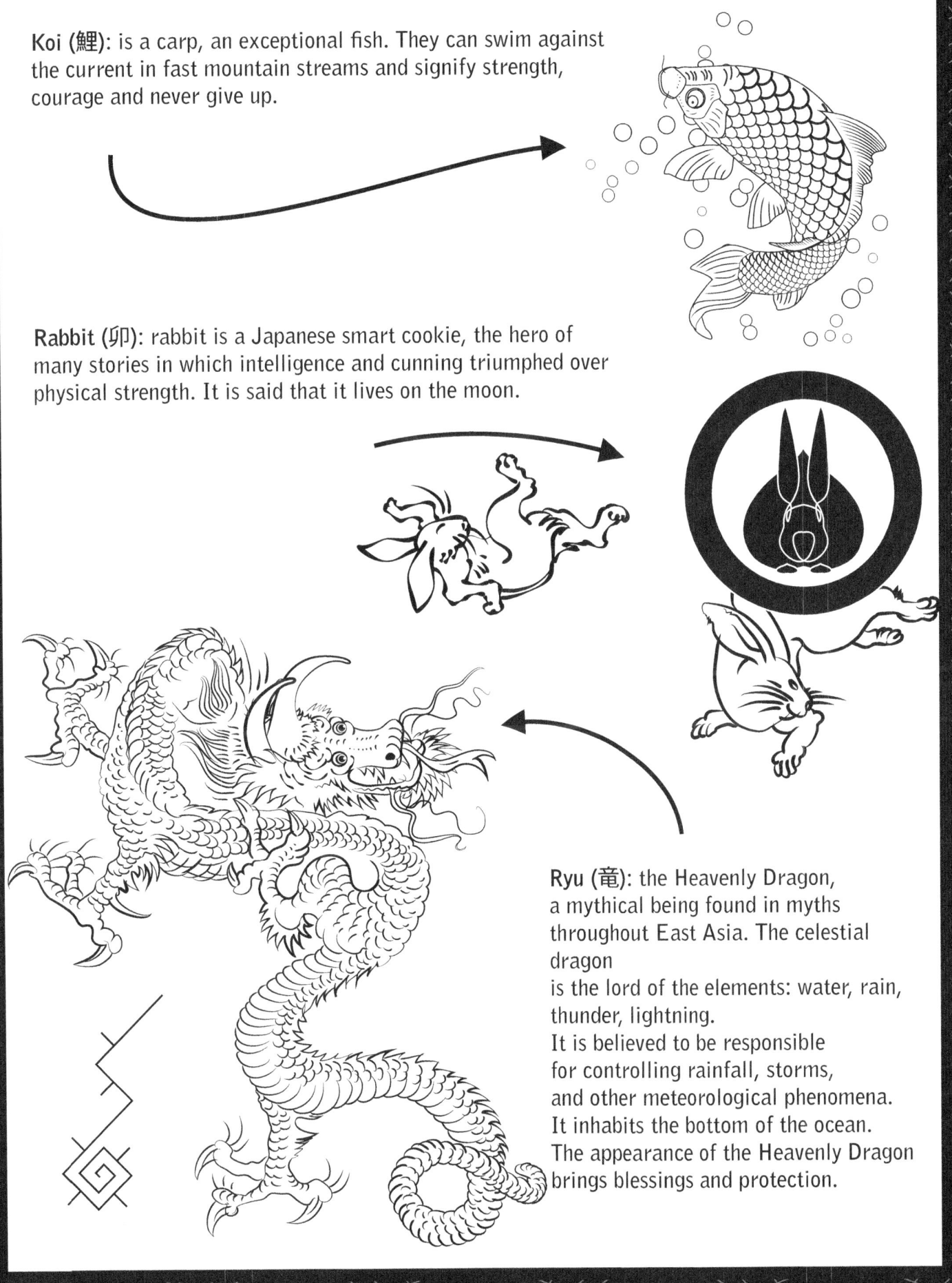

Koi (鯉): is a carp, an exceptional fish. They can swim against the current in fast mountain streams and signify strength, courage and never give up.

Rabbit (卯): rabbit is a Japanese smart cookie, the hero of many stories in which intelligence and cunning triumphed over physical strength. It is said that it lives on the moon.

Ryu (竜): the Heavenly Dragon, a mythical being found in myths throughout East Asia. The celestial dragon is the lord of the elements: water, rain, thunder, lightning.
It is believed to be responsible for controlling rainfall, storms, and other meteorological phenomena. It inhabits the bottom of the ocean. The appearance of the Heavenly Dragon brings blessings and protection.

Shippo (七宝): this geometric pattern consisting of intertwining circles forming a network refers to the seven stones of Buddhism and the related virtues of the human soul. The pattern originated in China about 100 years ago and is one of the oldest patterns used to decorate fabrics.

Sayagata (紗綾形): it is an unusual geometric pattern, a Japanese Meander. The breaking lines form a labyrinth. The pattern symbolizes difficult and intricate path to the goal. It is closely related to Buddhism.

Another interesting Japanese feature is **Kamon (家紋)** – these are like family emblems. In the old days, they were used to show which family or group a person belonged to, and it was important in battles. Nowadays, they are used more as symbols representing their culture and history.

Among the most famous are:
Go-shichi-no-kiri,
Kikko-Chrysanthemum,
Tokugawa,
Gomaisa
Mitsugashiwa,
Tomoe,
Ashikaga
and others.

These motifs are made in various ways, such as weaving, embroidery, painting using the yuzen-zome technique and decorating using the Kata-zome method. Often the different techniques were used simultaneously. The yuzen technique or hand-painting on silk. It is a unique technique and therefore expensive. Only the wealthiest could afford a kimono decorated with the yuzen method.

All these patterns constitute a large part of Japanese culture and history, used not only in and clothing but also in architecture, crafts and art.

It's fascinating!

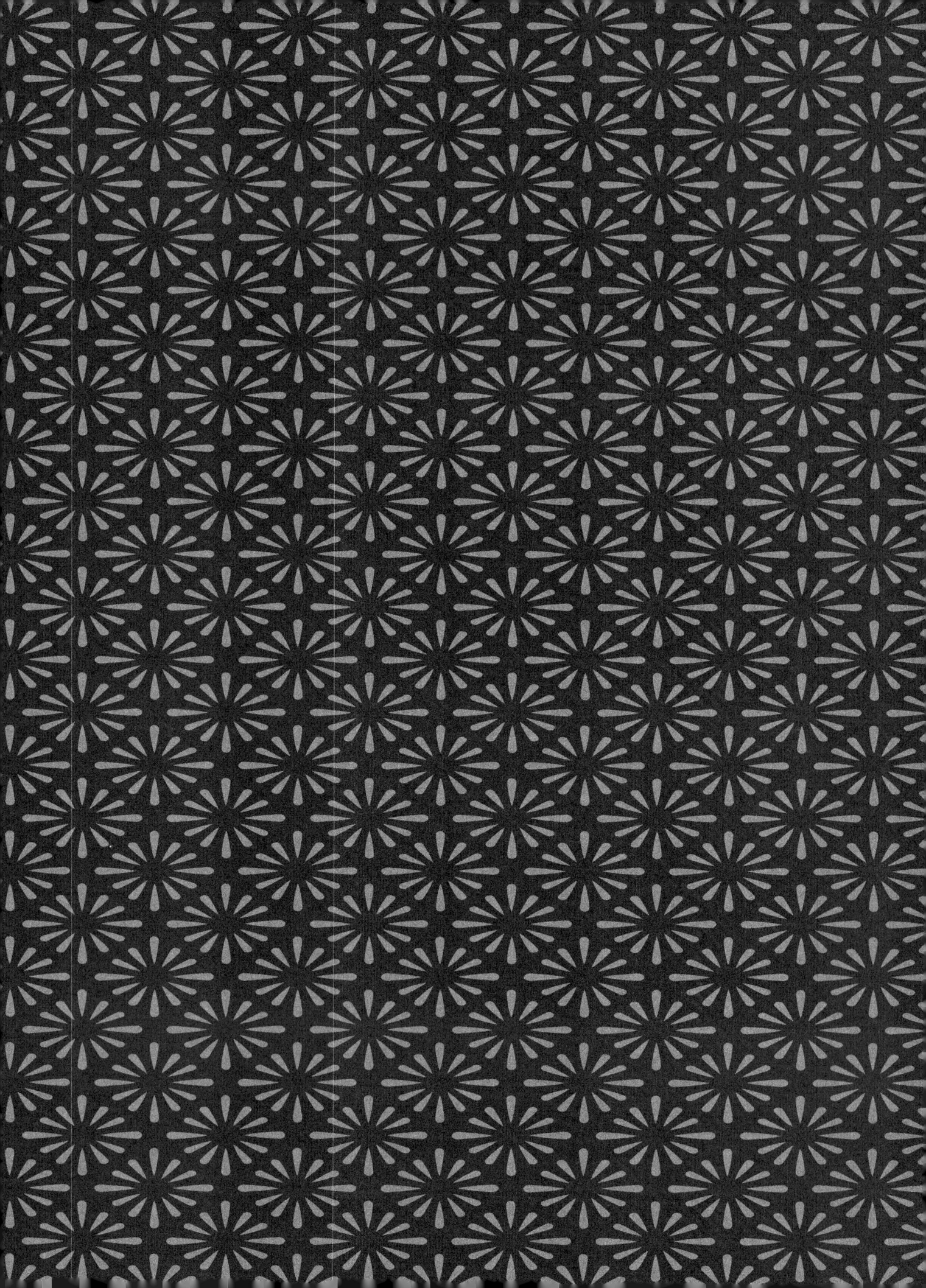

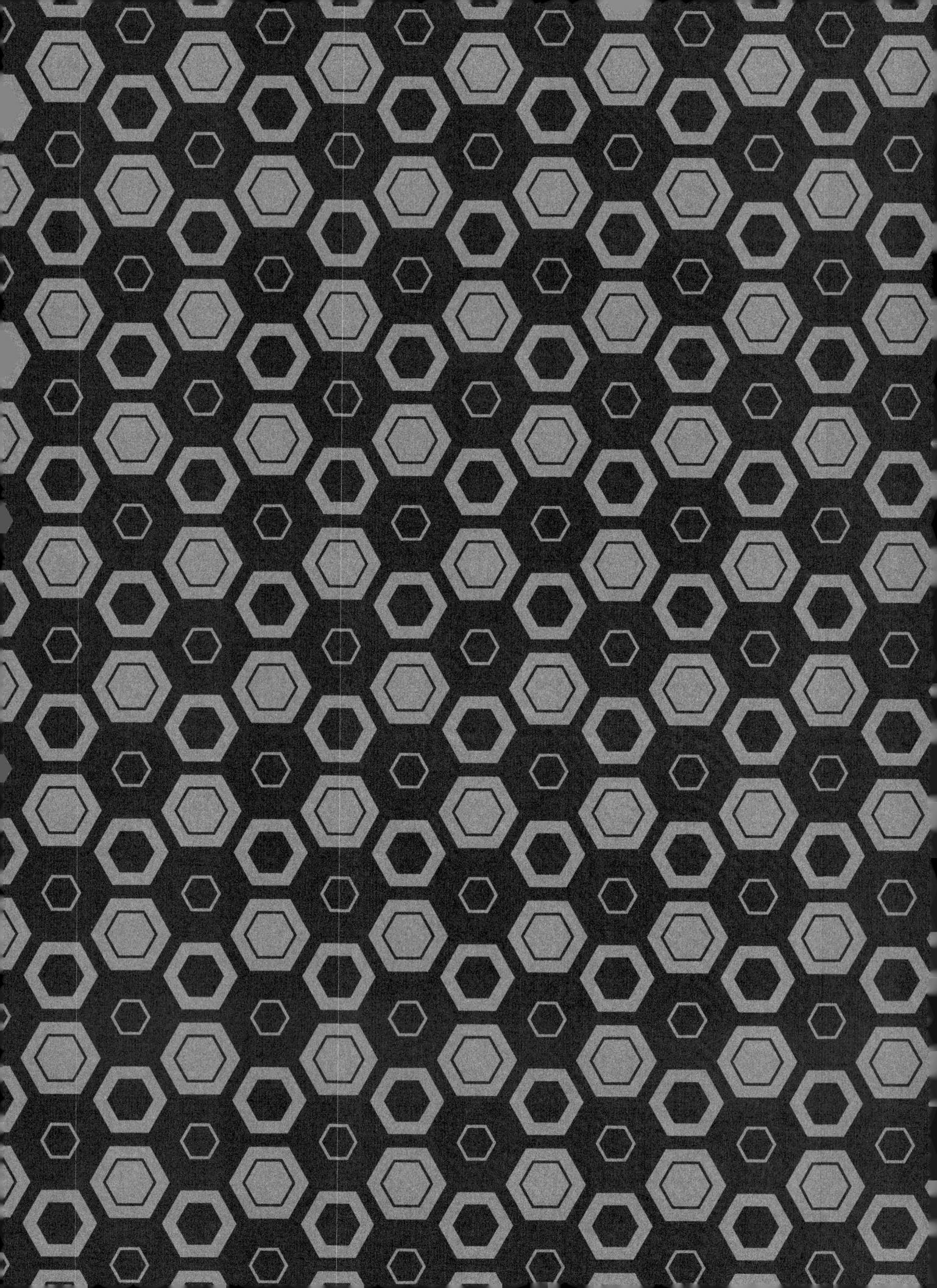

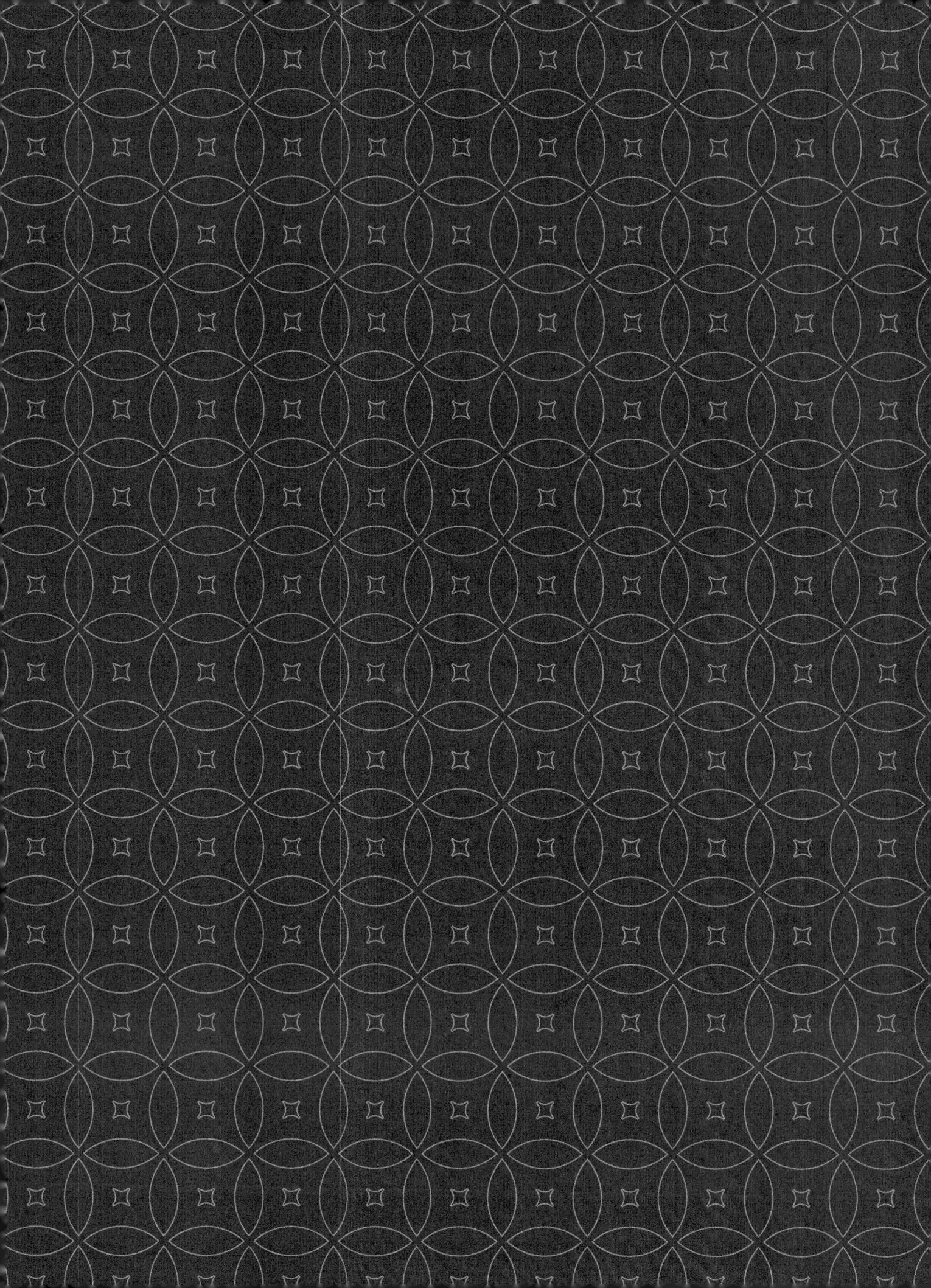

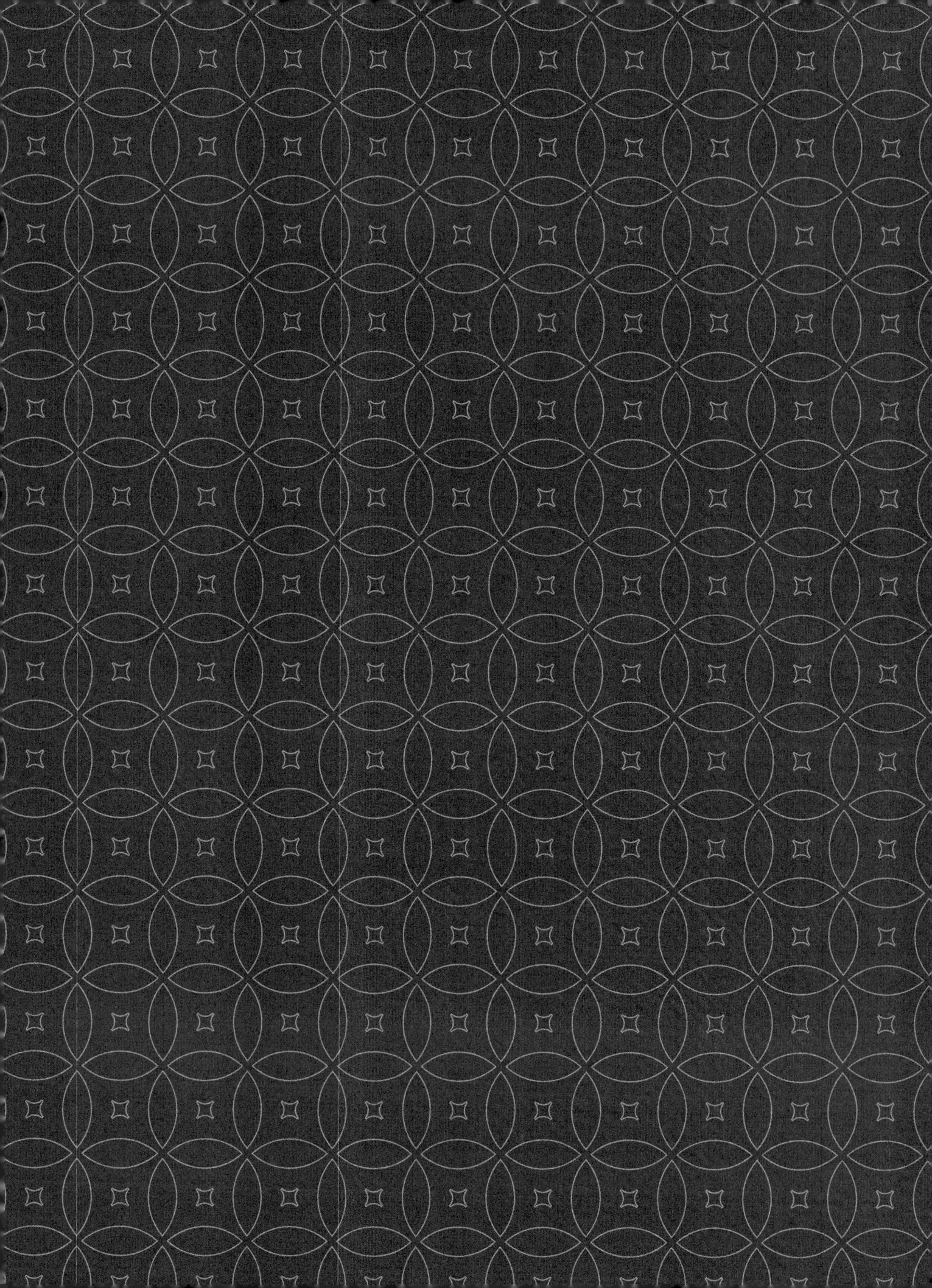

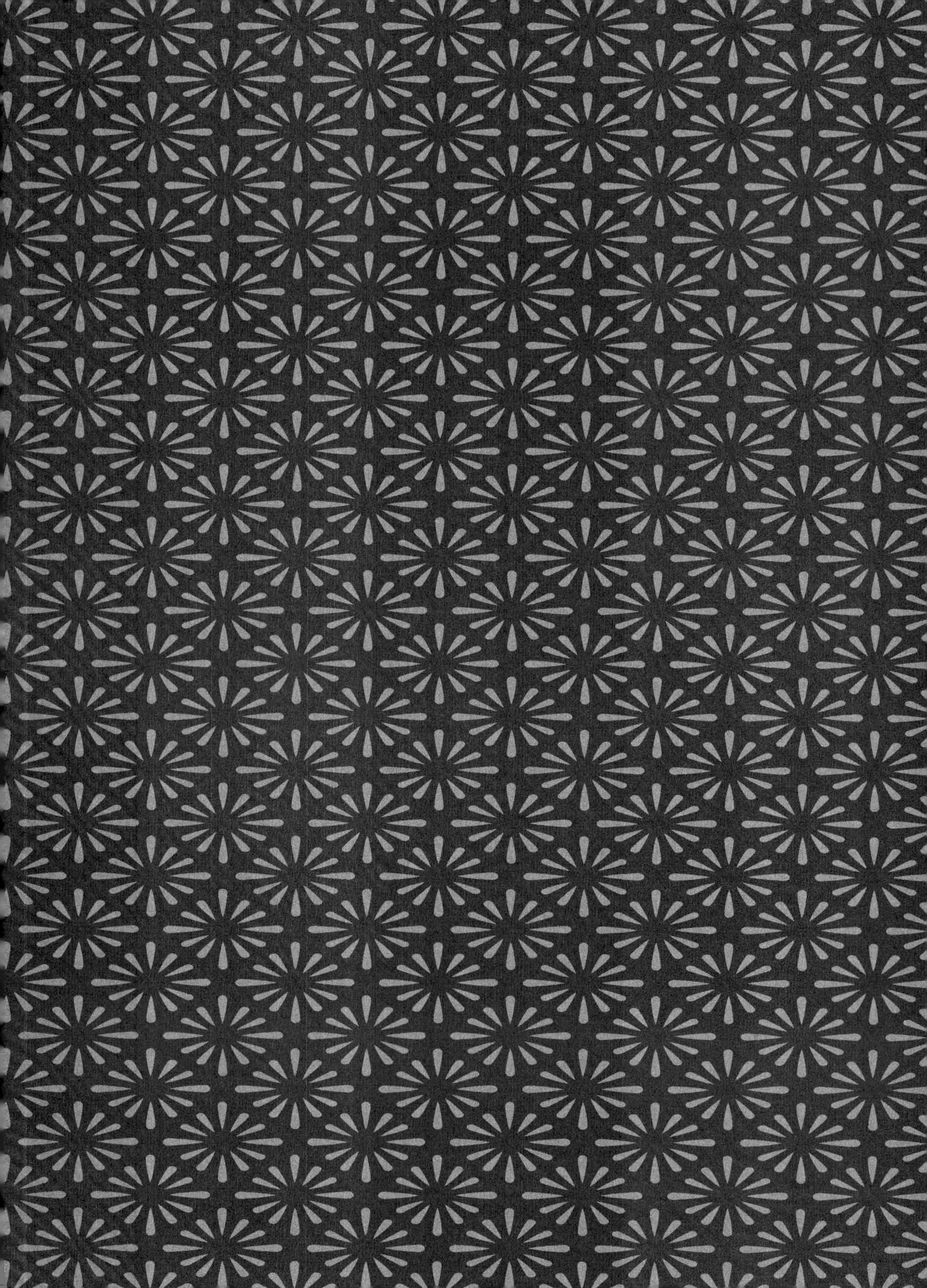

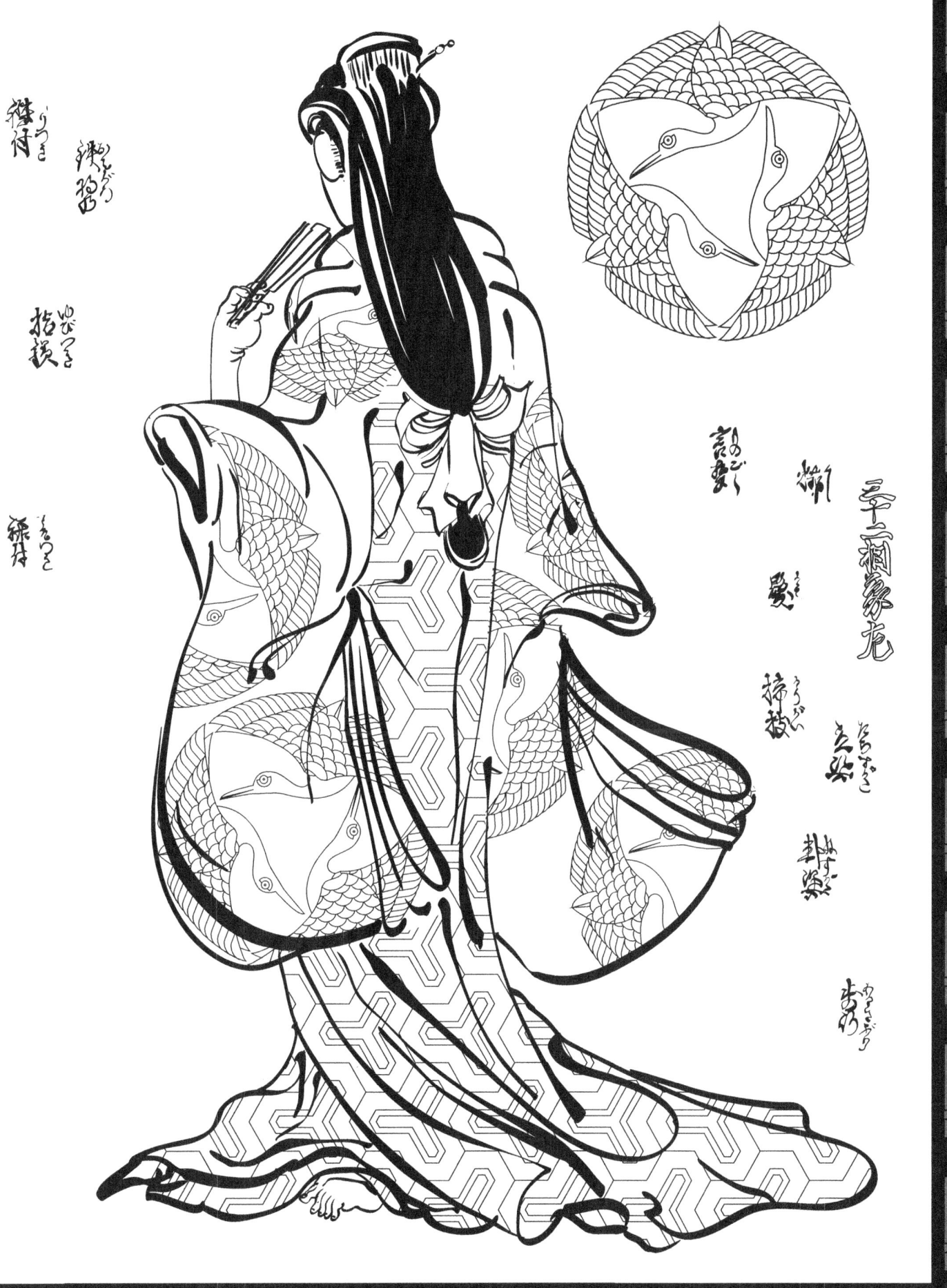

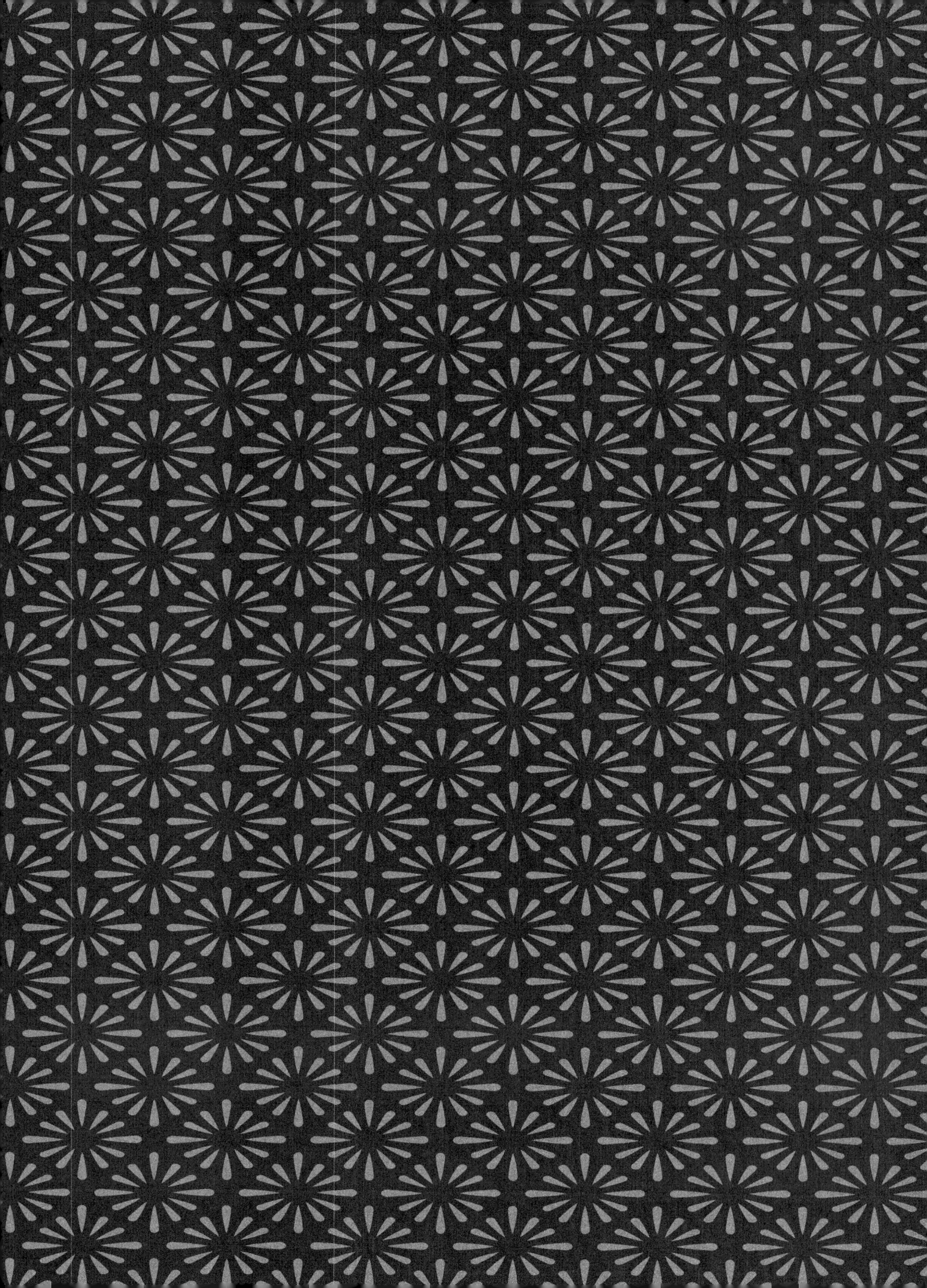

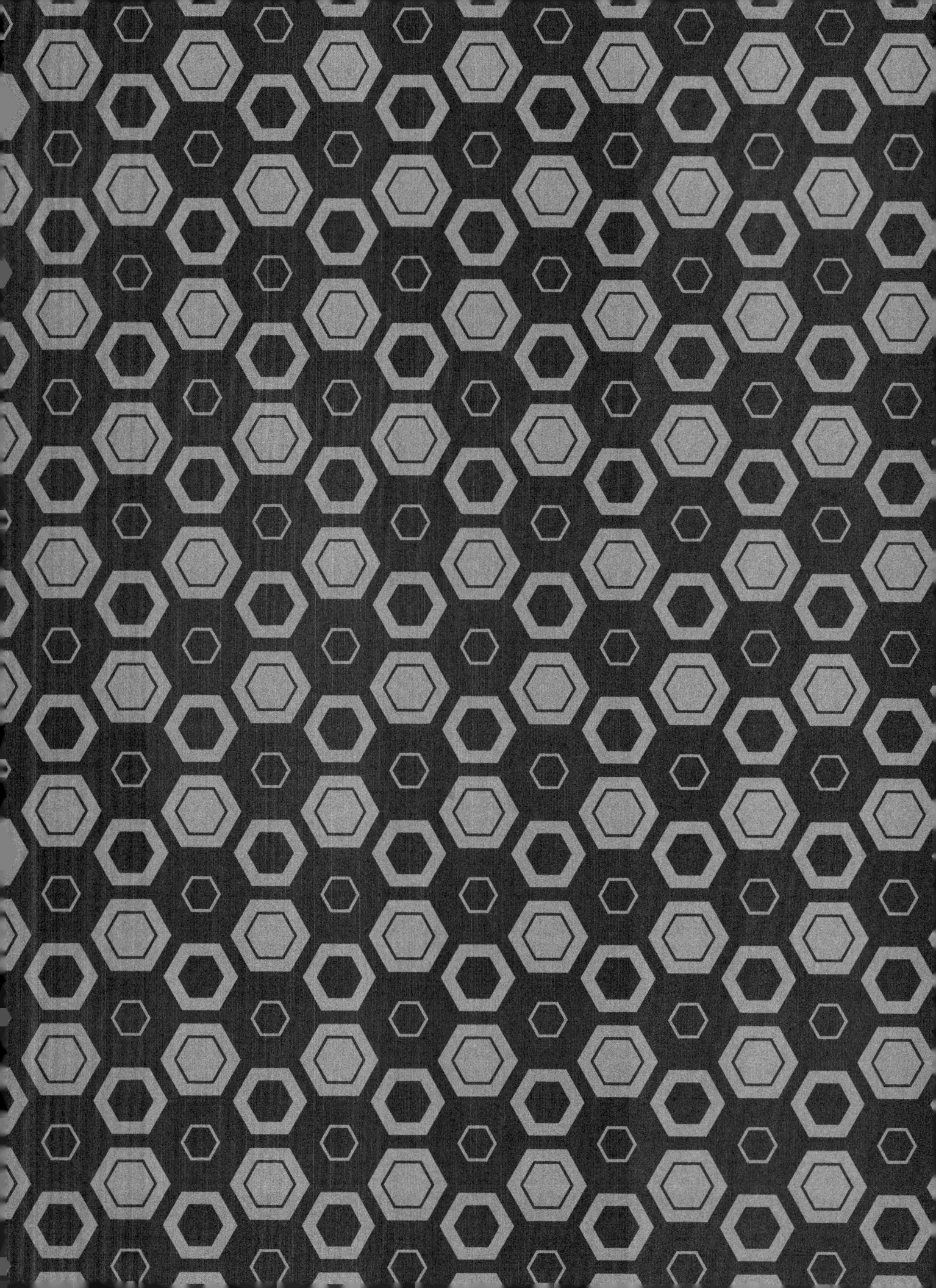

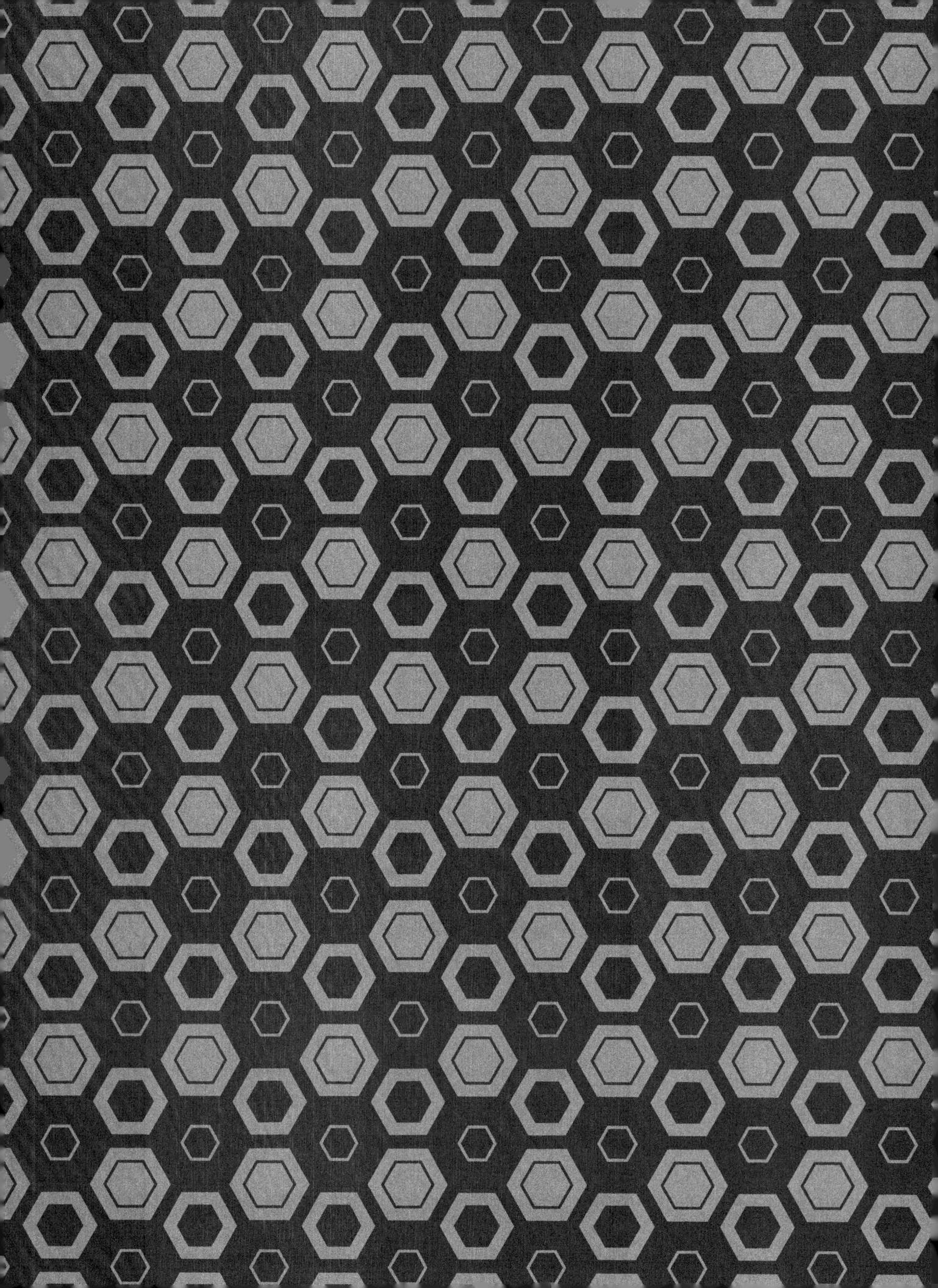

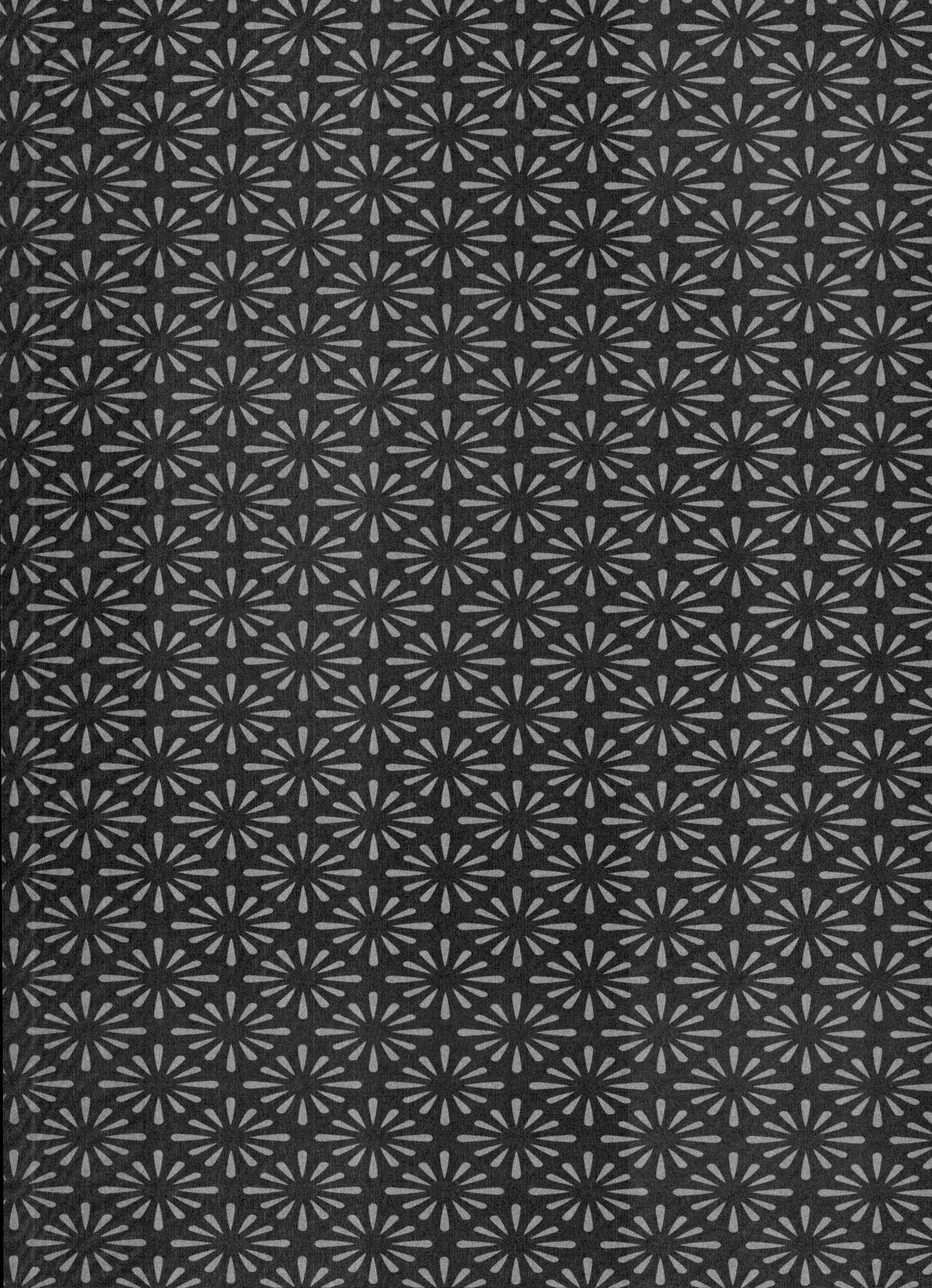

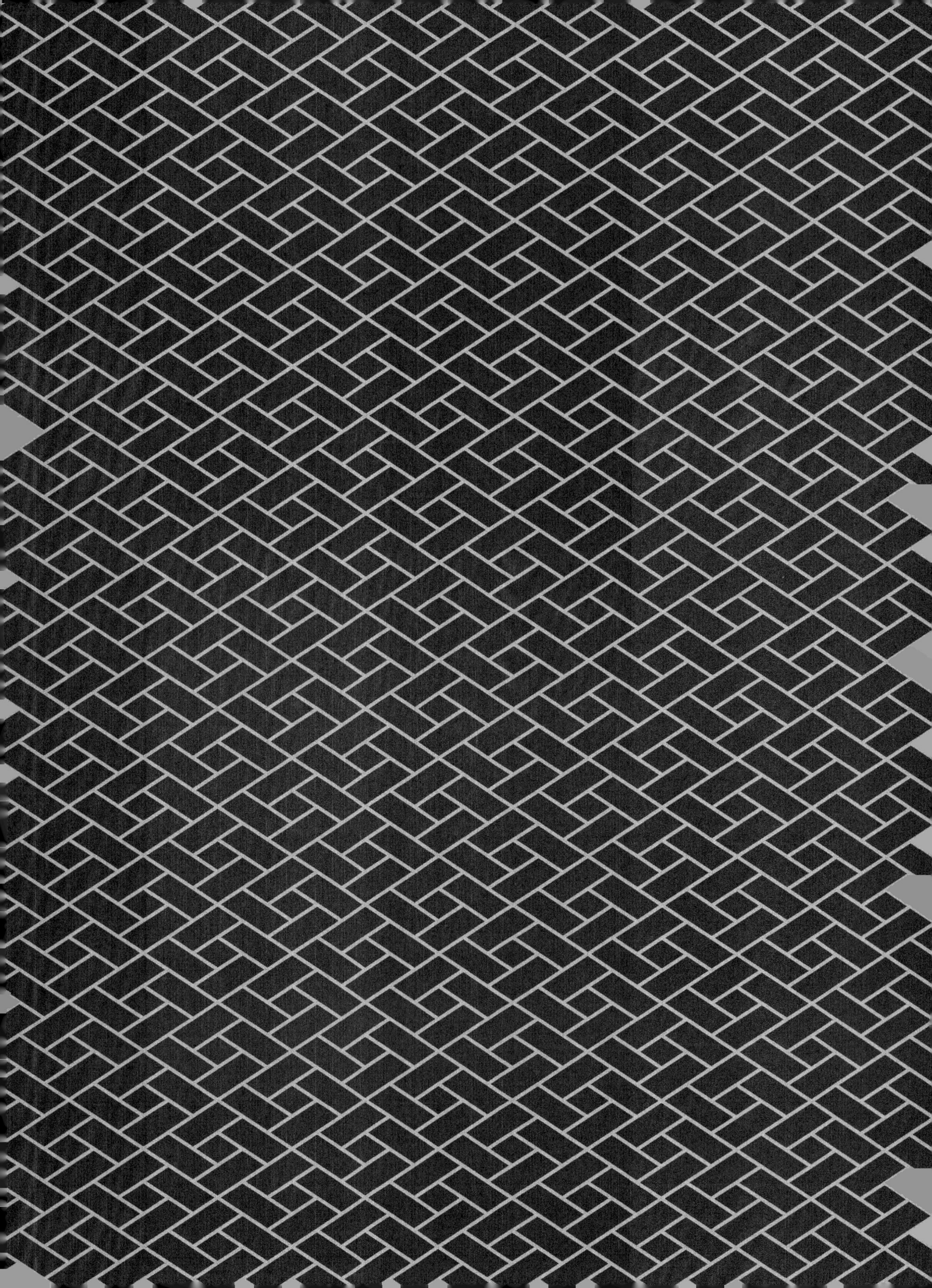

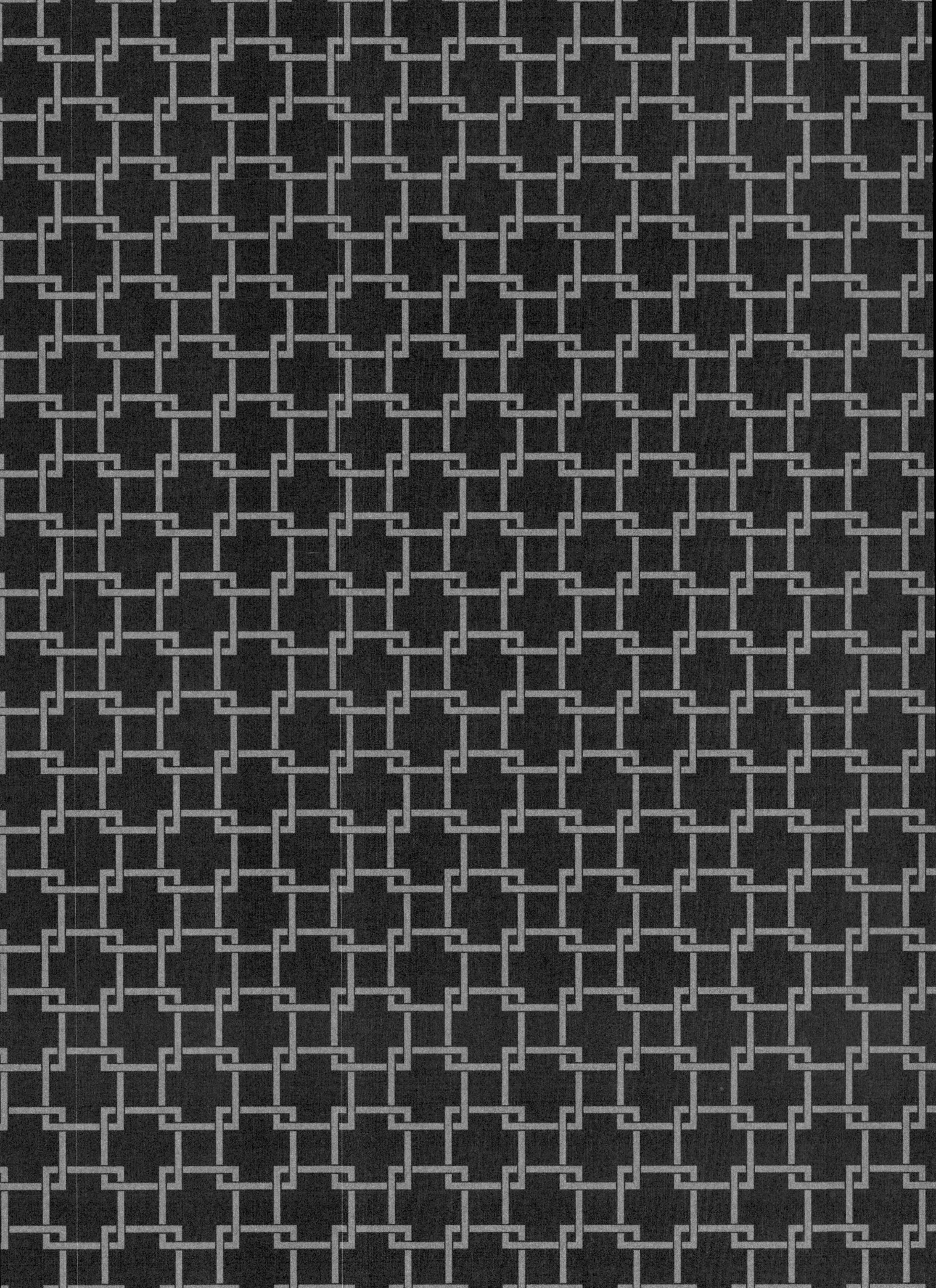

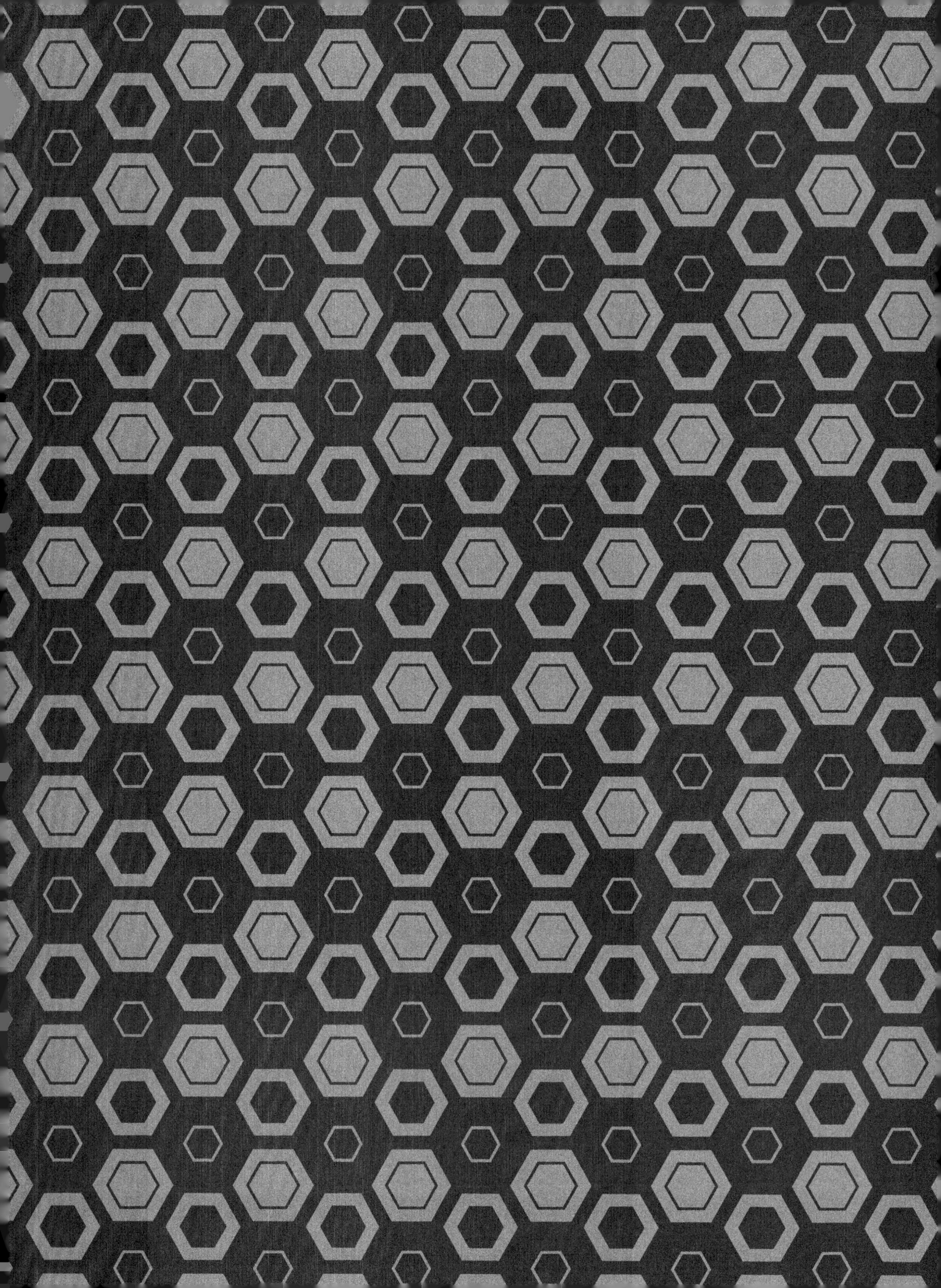

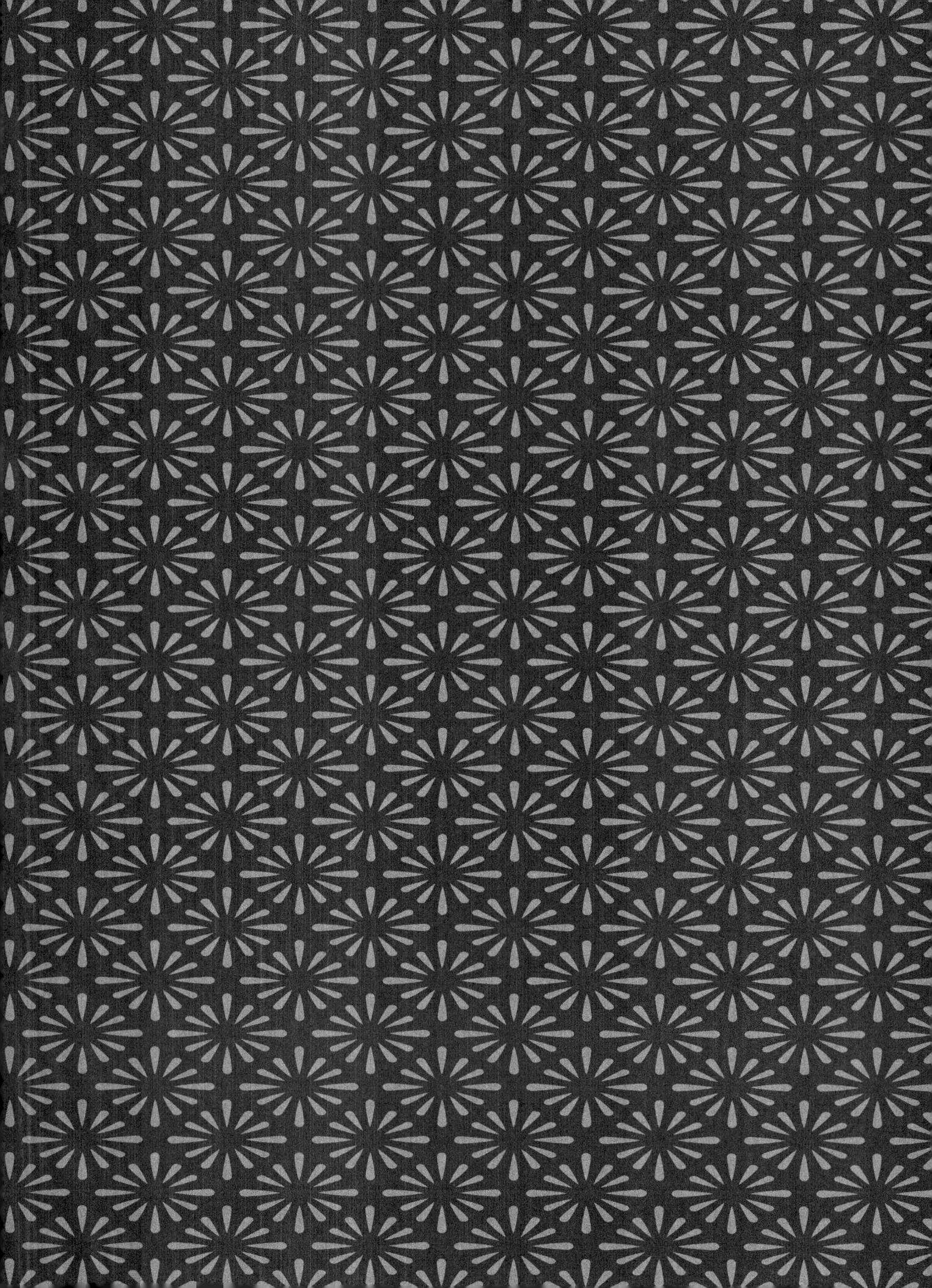

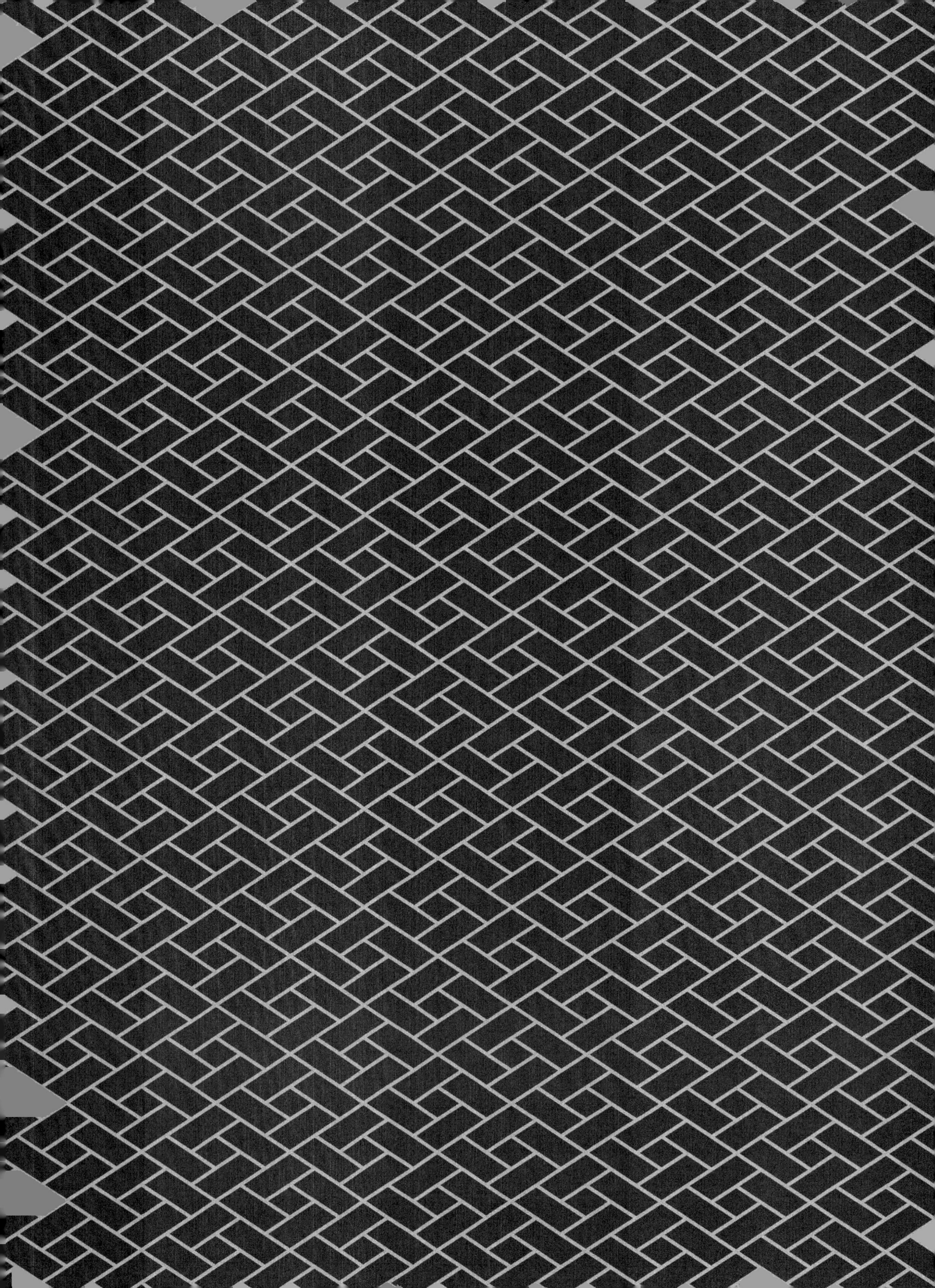

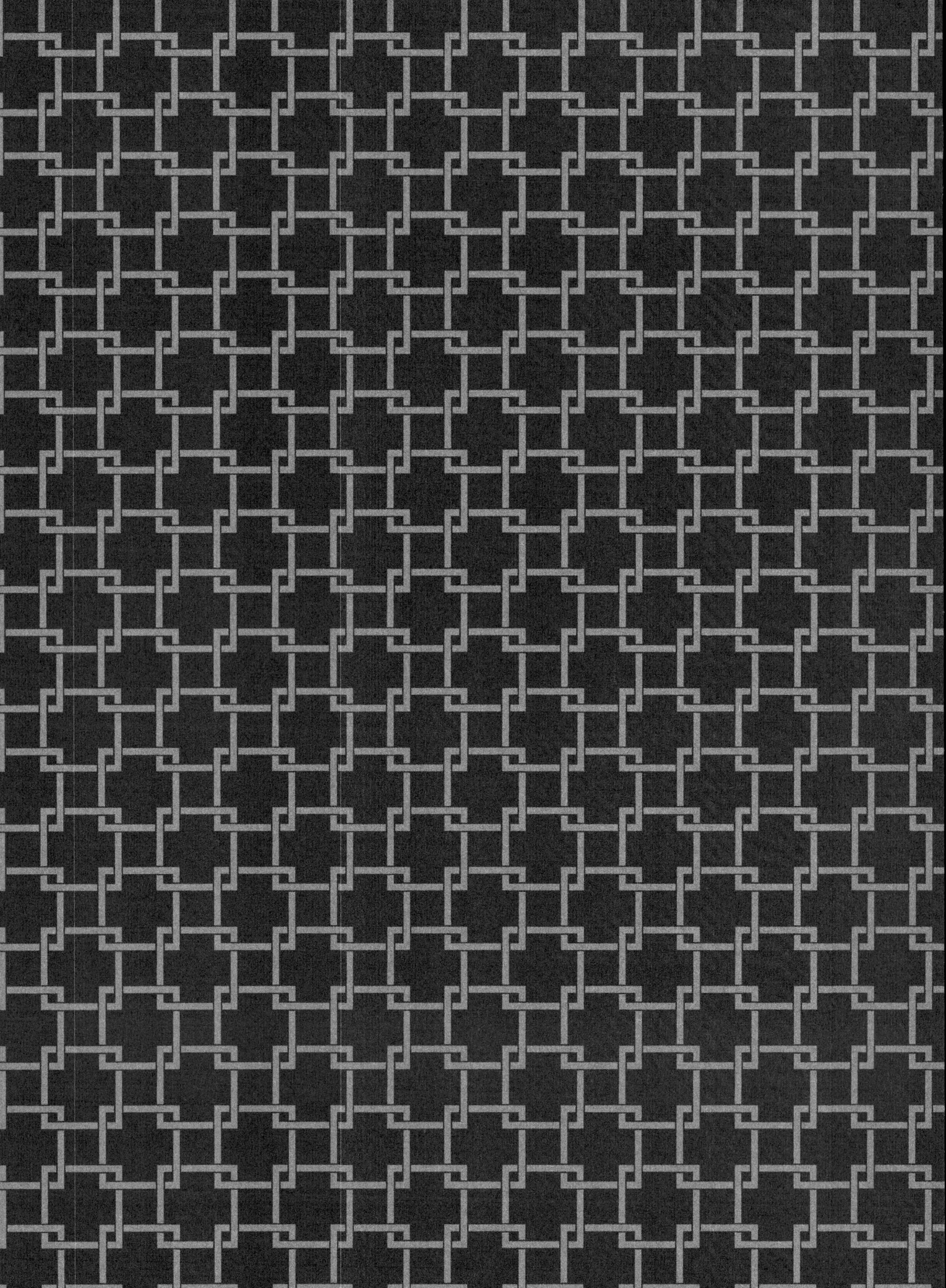

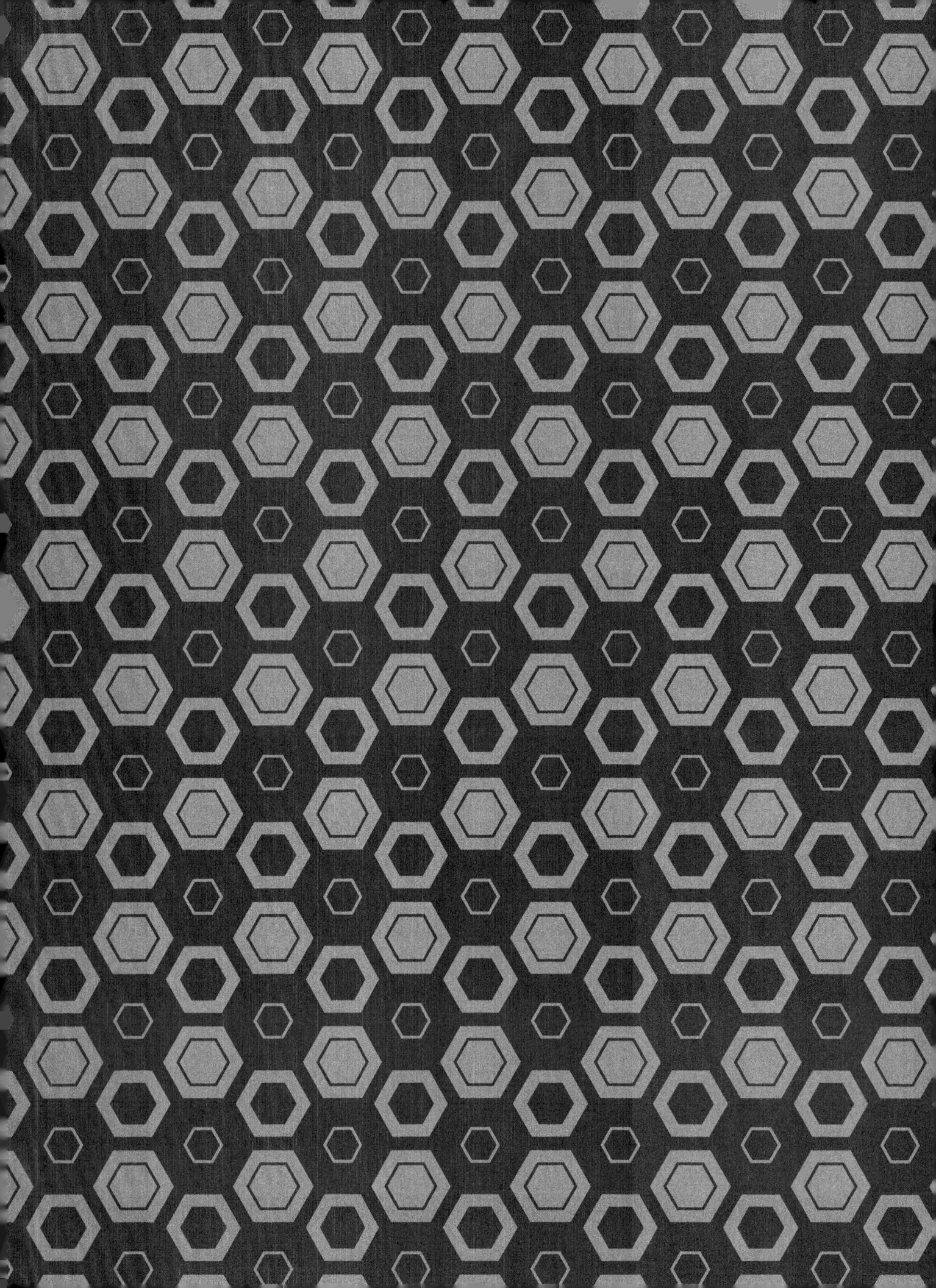

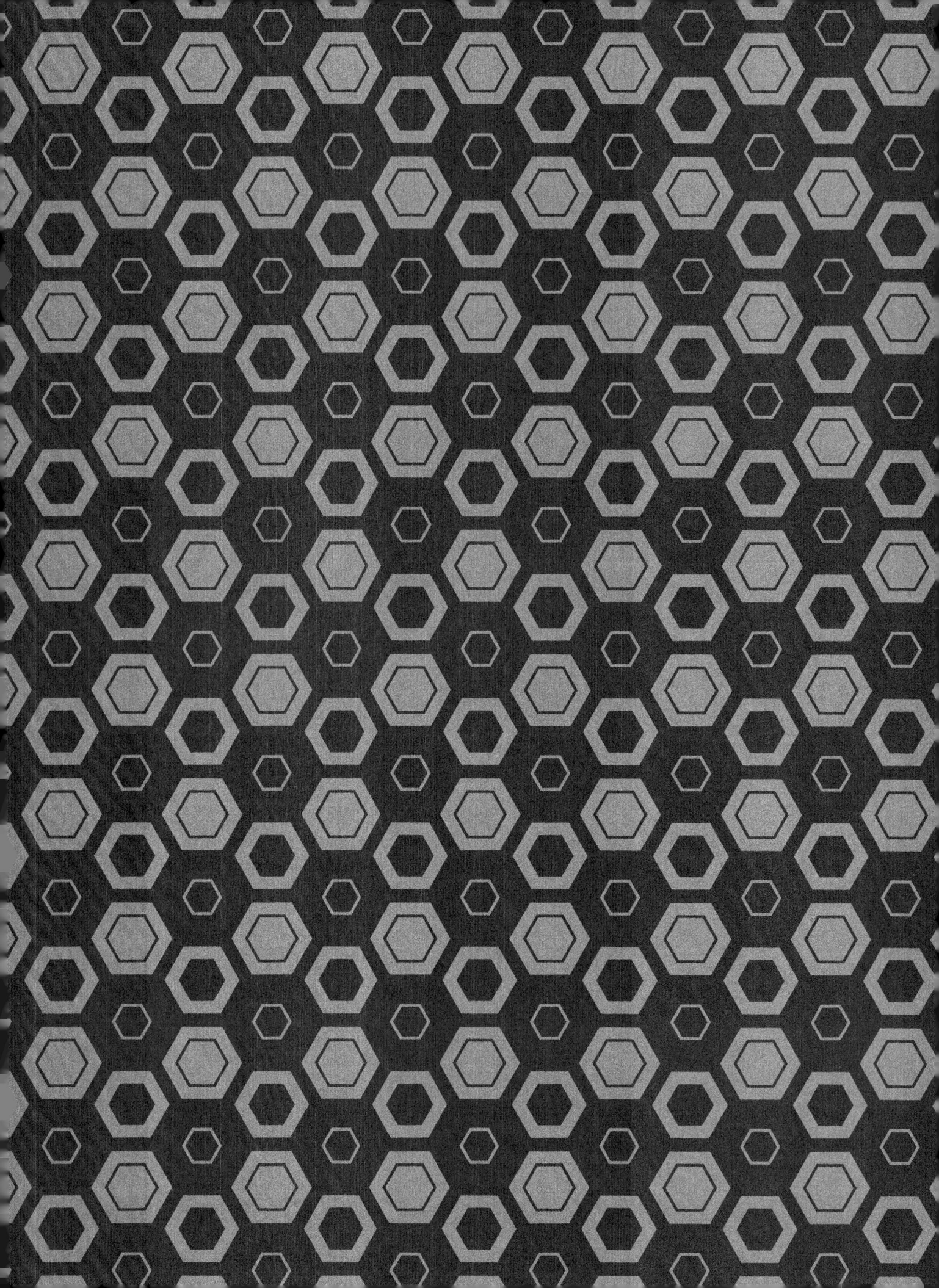

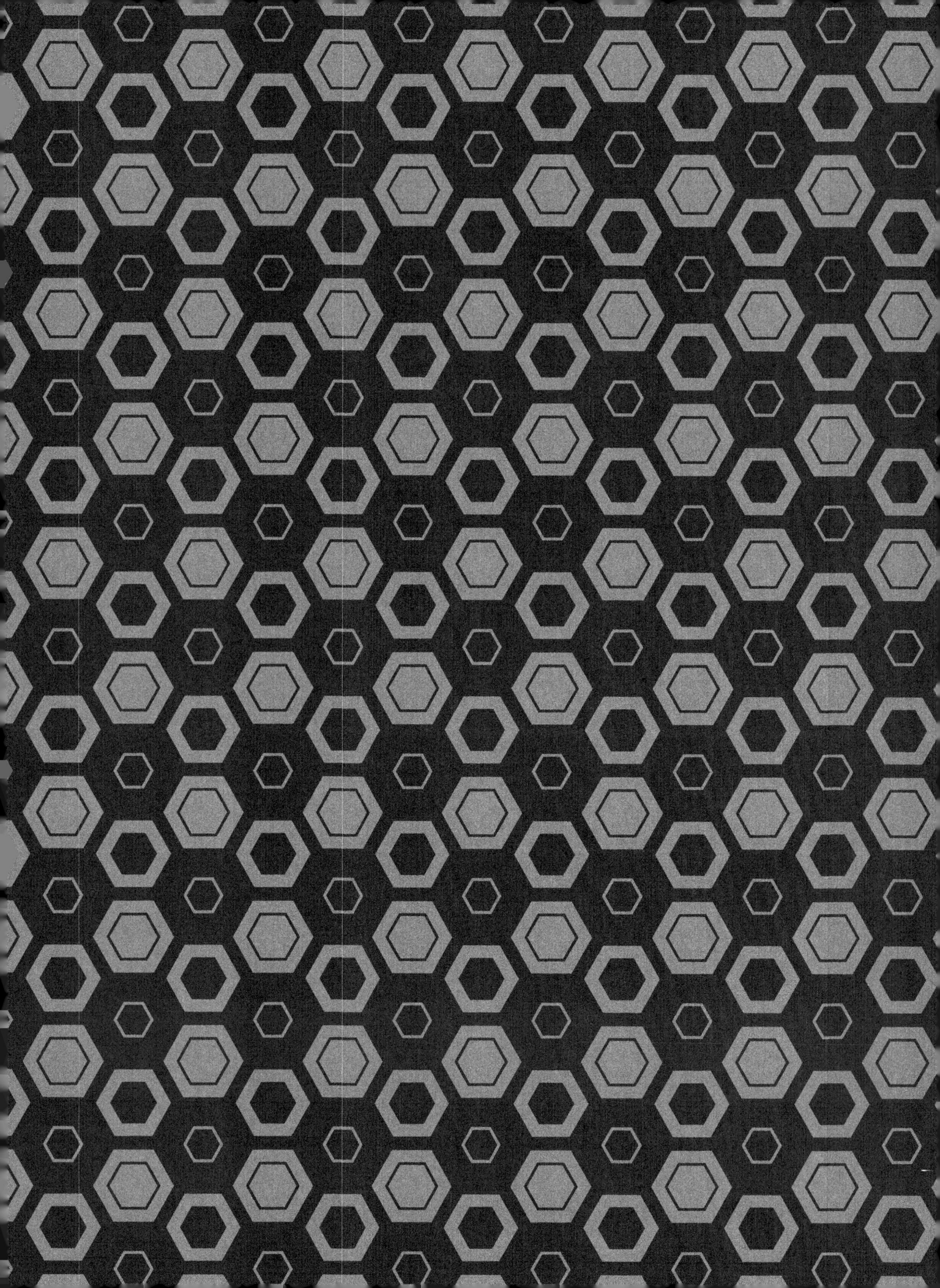

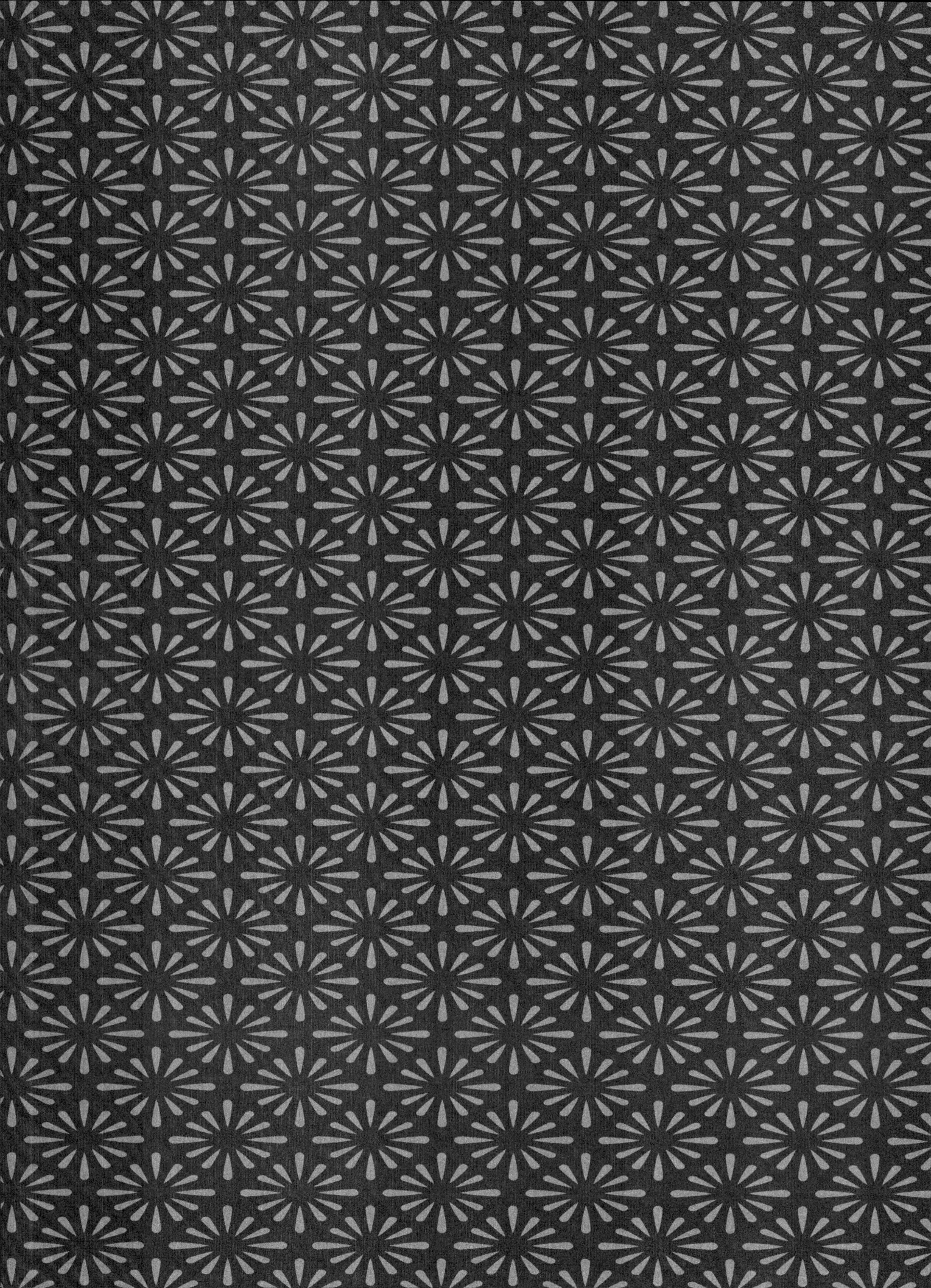

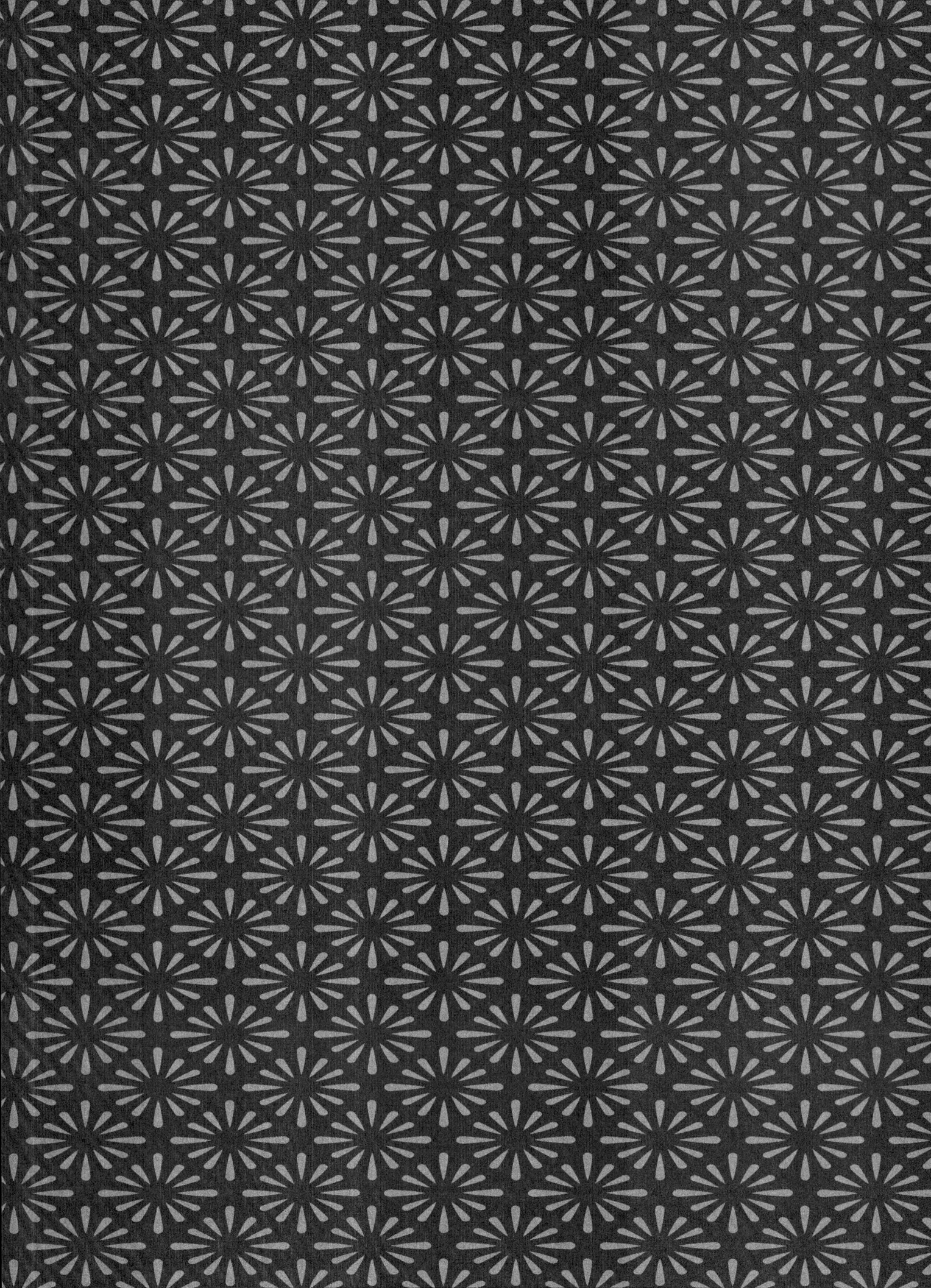

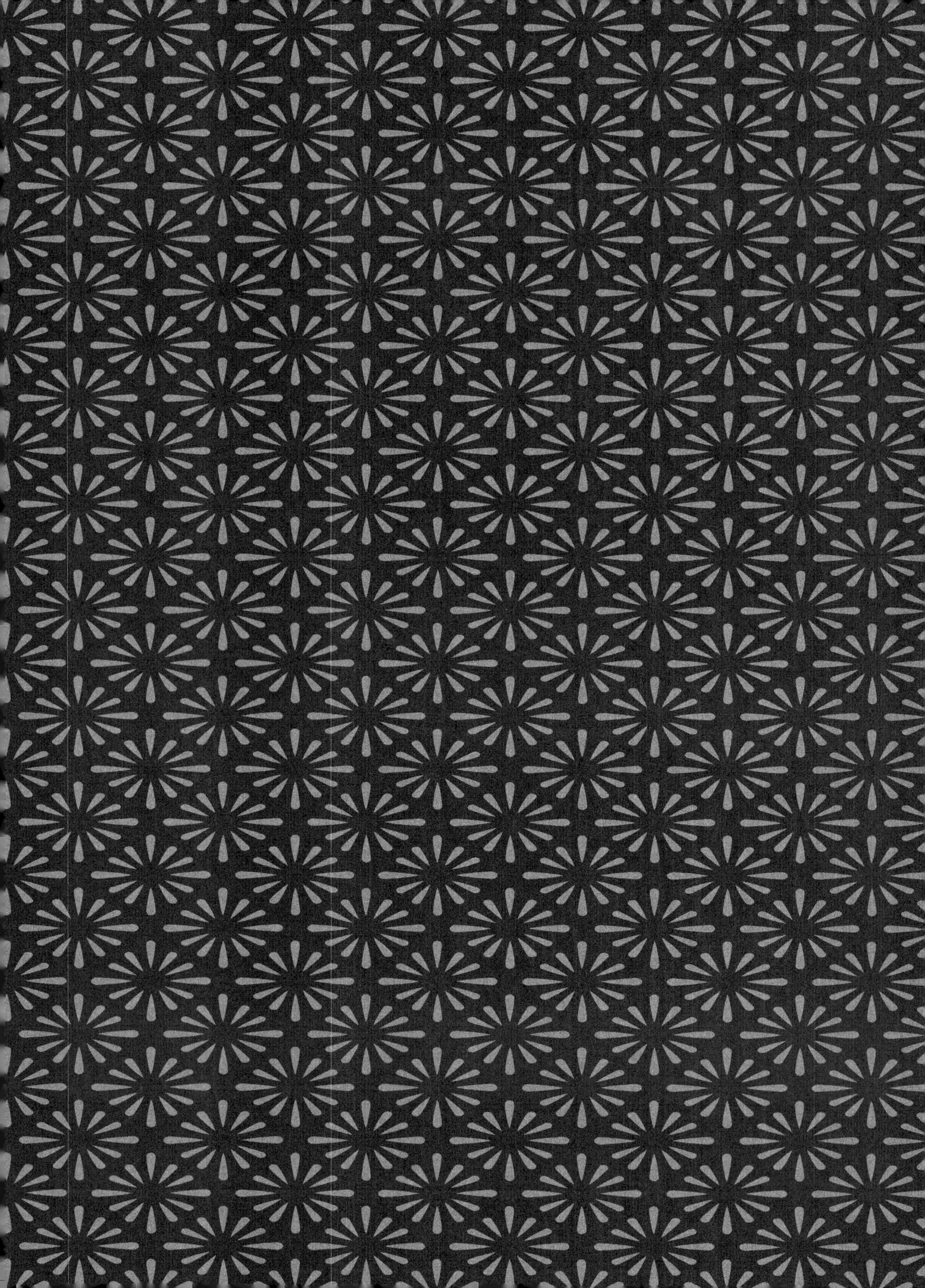

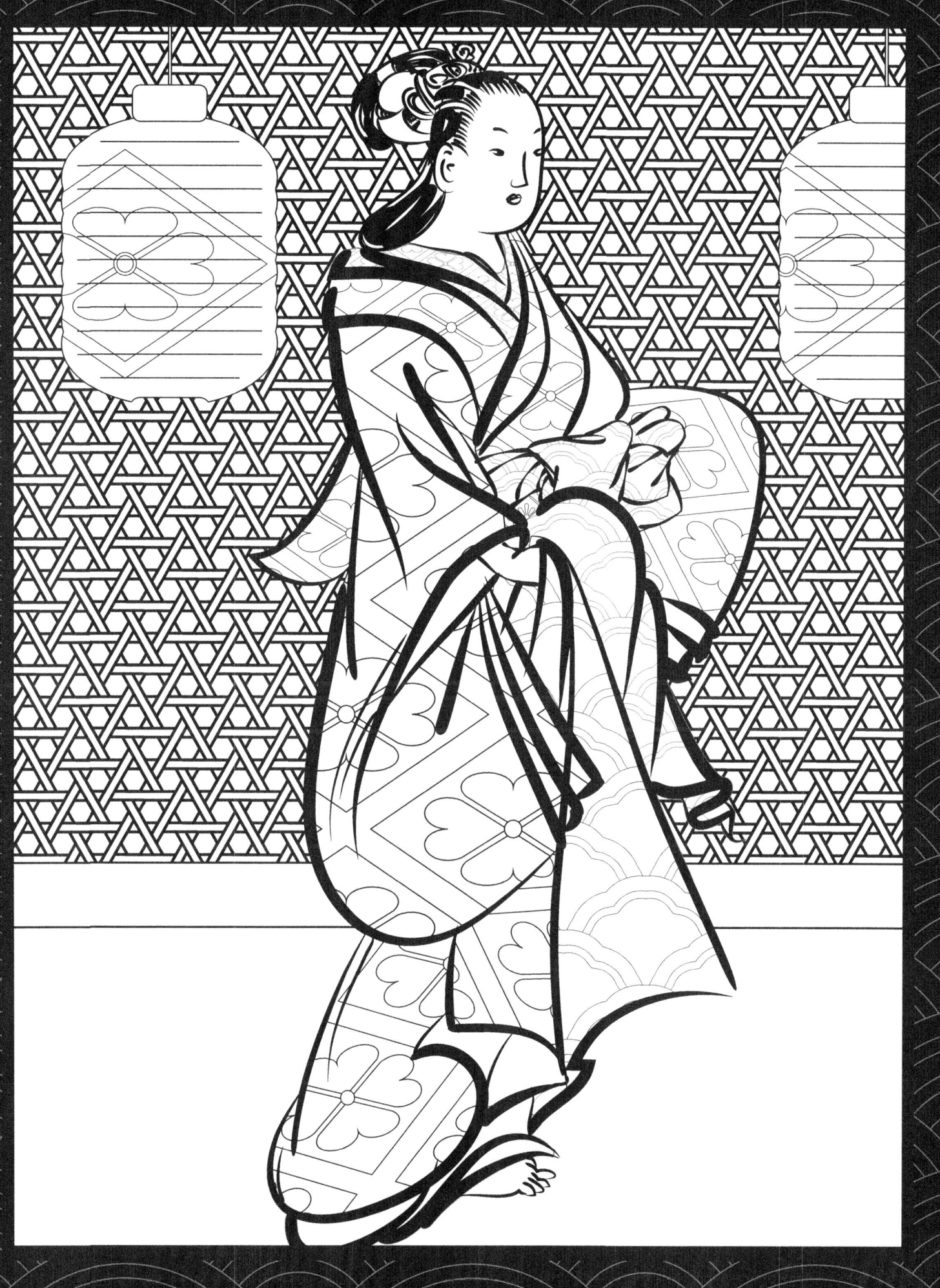

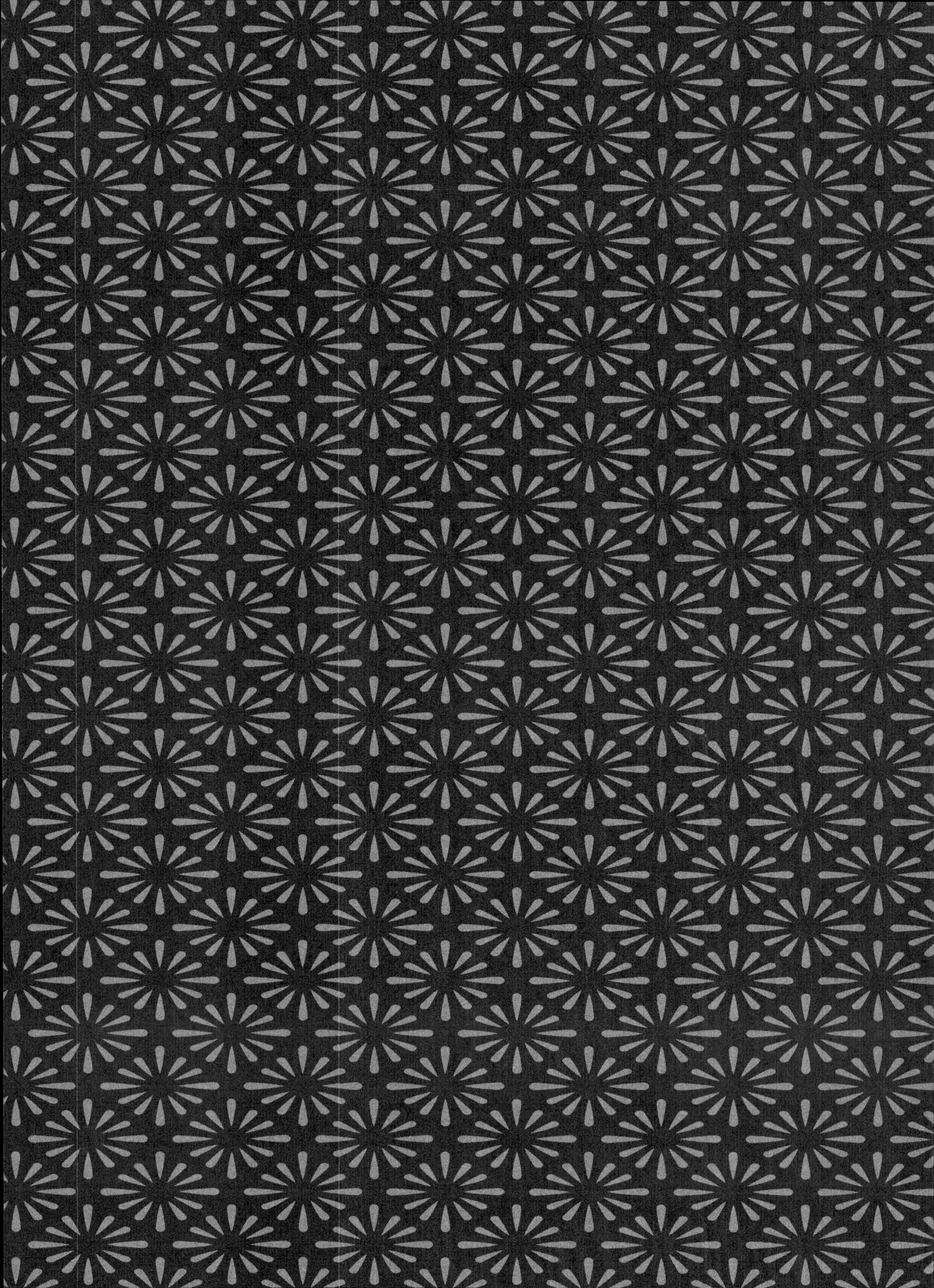

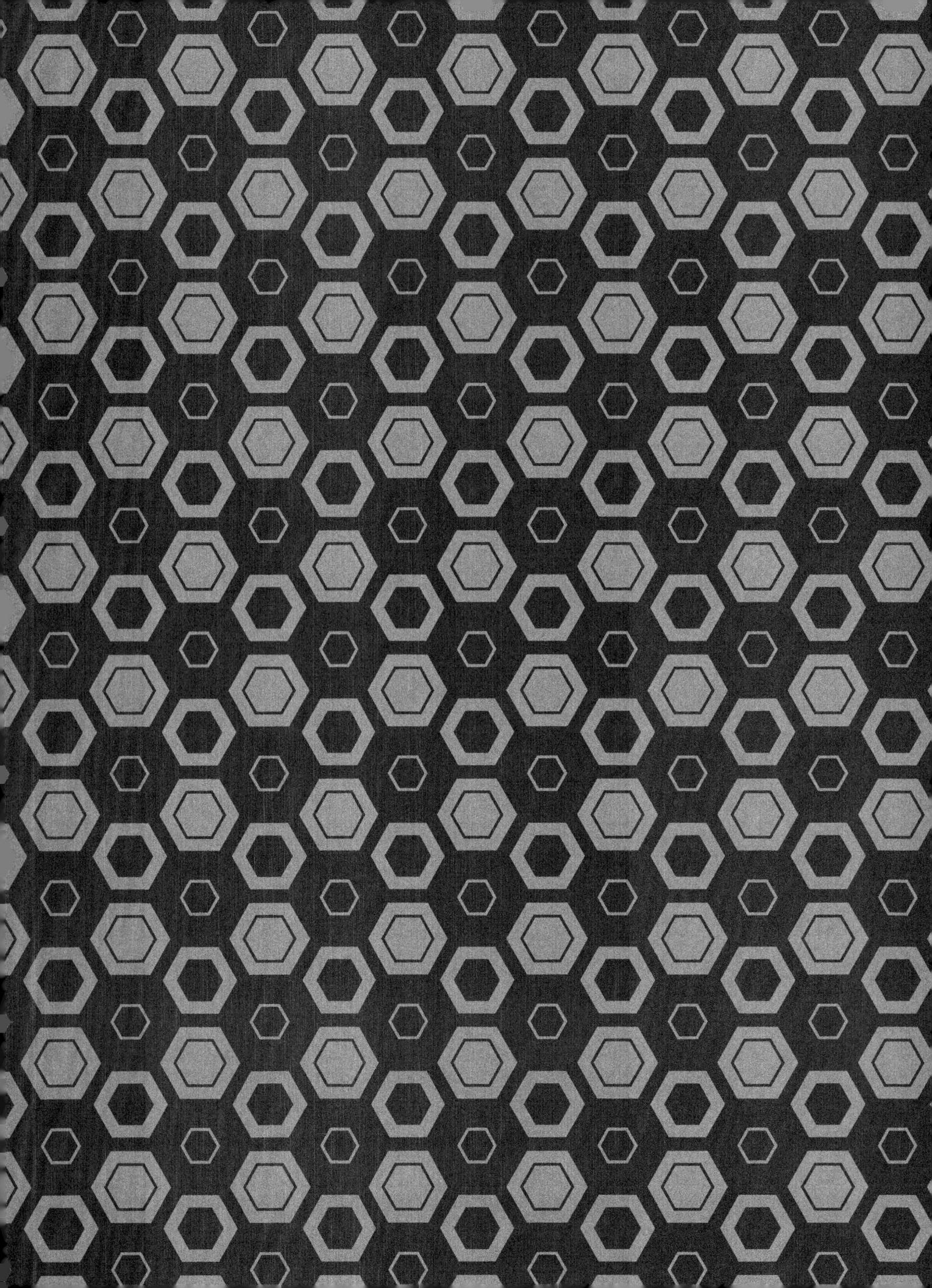

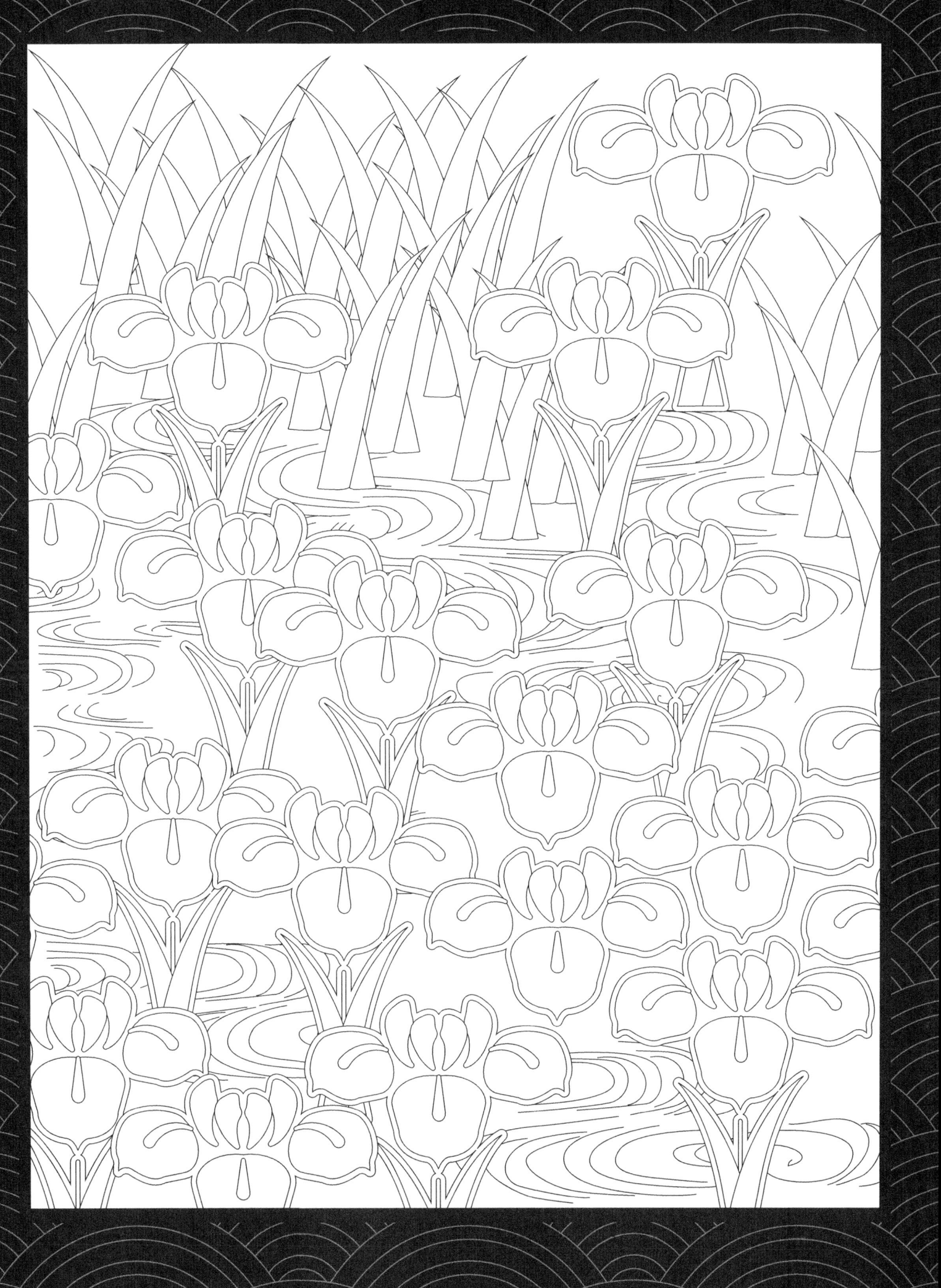

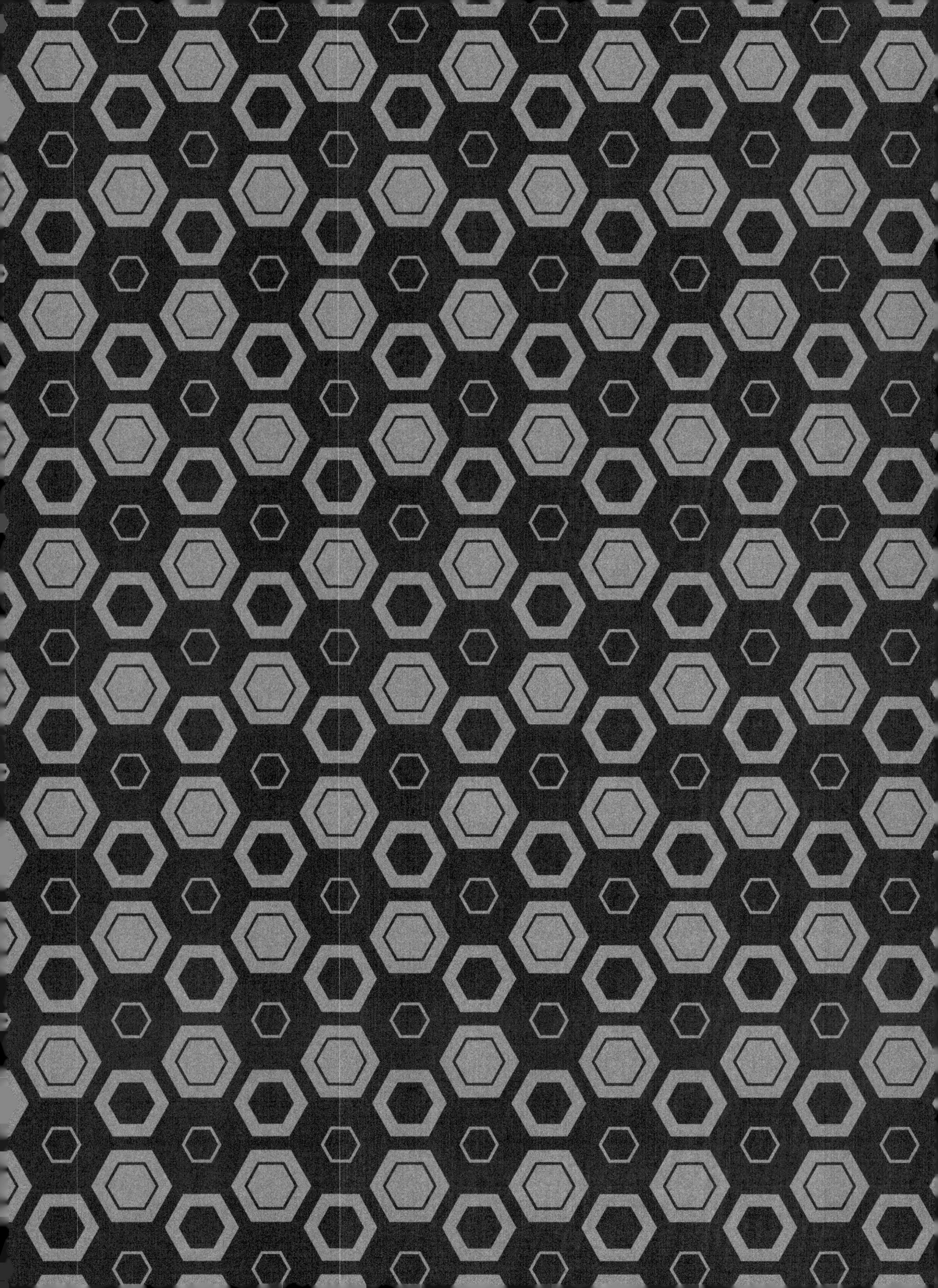

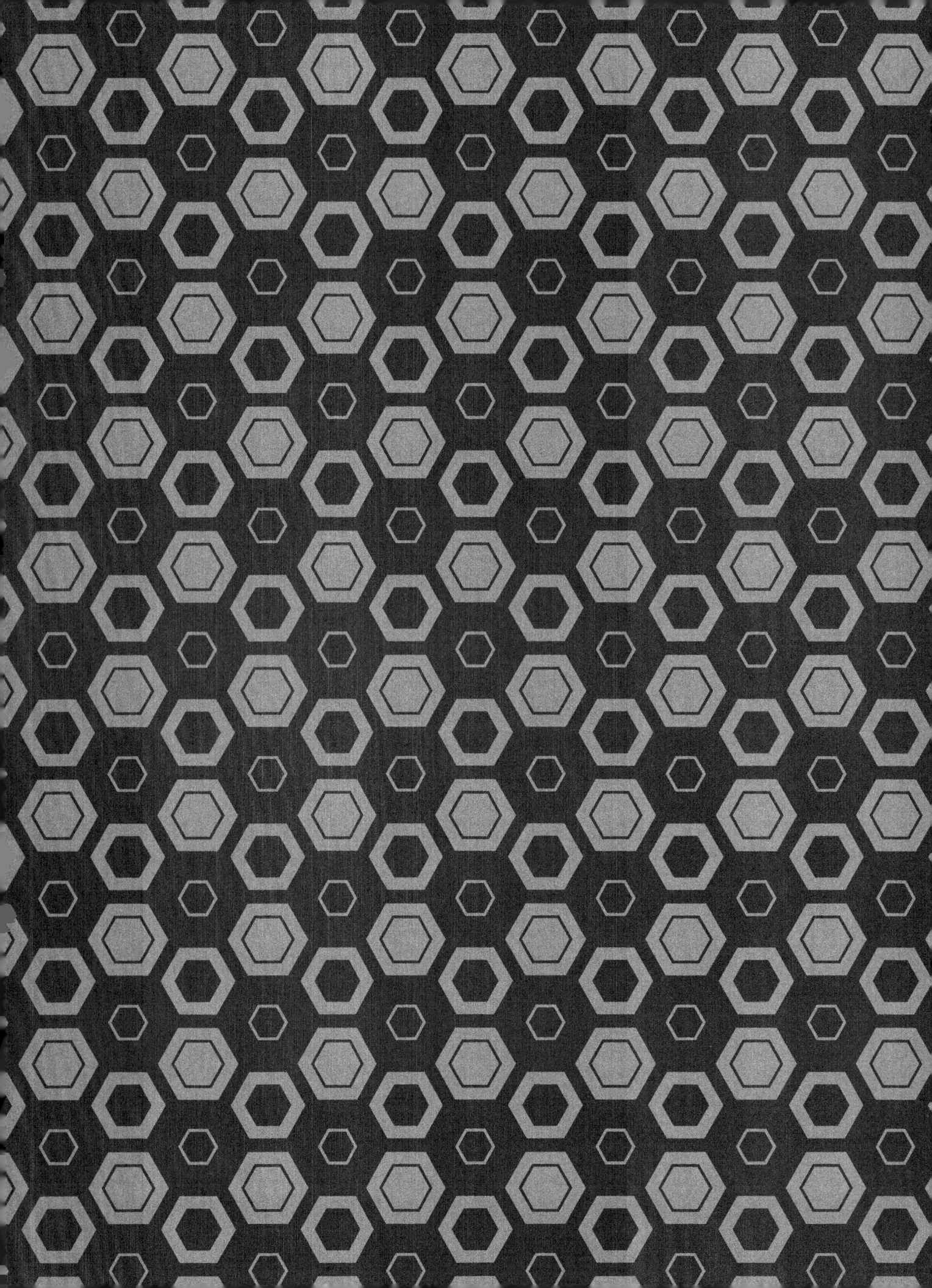

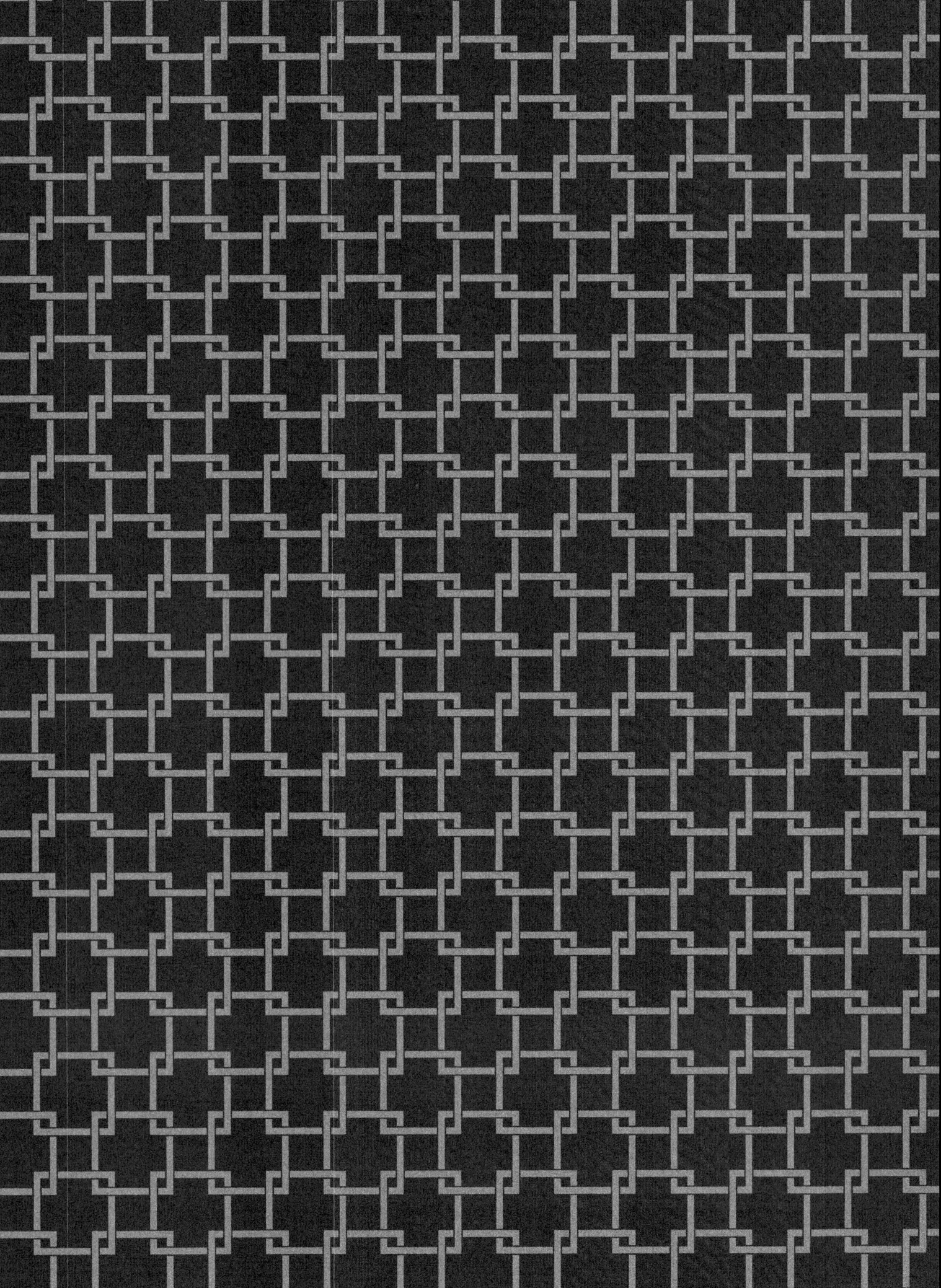

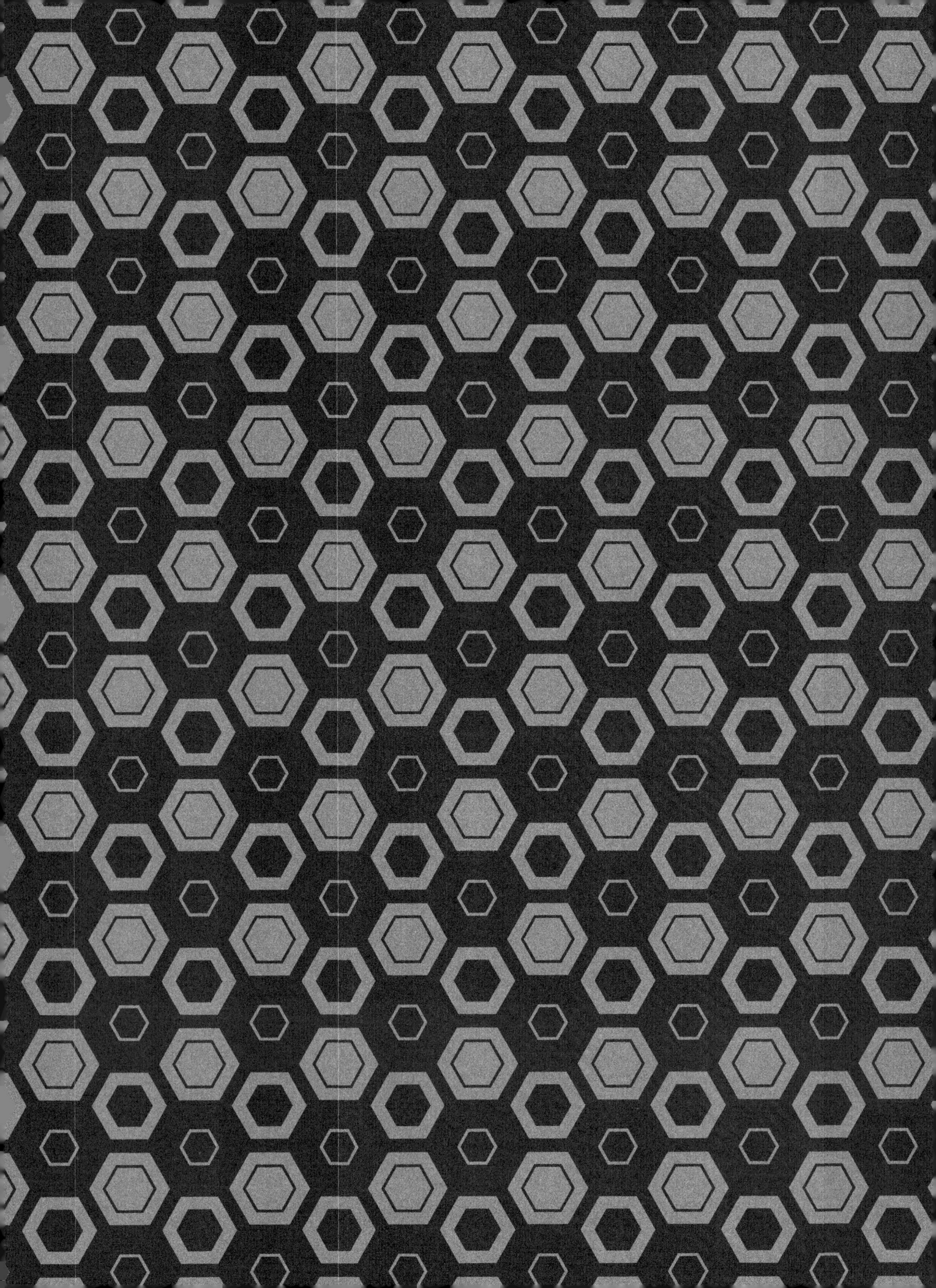